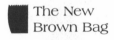

The New
Brown Bag

Growing Seeds of Faith

The New
Brown Bag

Growing Seeds of Faith

Virginia H. Loewen

THE
PILGRIM
PRESS
Cleveland

To Benjamin David, Matthew James, Lisa Marie, and Steven William with a prayer that, as you grow in years, you will continue to grow in faith and in wisdom by walking with God.

The Pilgrim Press, 700 Prospect Avenue East
Cleveland, Ohio 44115-1100
pilgrimpress.com

Printed in the United States of America on acid-free paper

06 05 04 03 02   5 4 3 2 1

Library of Congress Cataloging-in-Publication Data

Loewen, Virginia H., 1932-
    Growing seeds of faith / Virginia H. Loewen.
        p.   cm.   (The new brown bag)
    Includes bibliographical references and index.
    ISBN 0-8298-1488-4 (alk. paper)
    1. Children's sermons.   I. Title.   II. Series

BV4315 .L58   2002
252'.53–dc21

2002031194

Contents

Preface

We are most impressionable when we are children. The attitudes, habits, concepts, and truths we learn when we are young stay with us throughout adulthood. *Growing Seeds of Faith*, a sequel to *Planting Seeds of Faith*, provides messages about God for children to establish firmly in their hearts that God loves them. Special attention is given to holidays and holy days occurring between June and November.

I am thankful for the efforts of field-testers Rev. Dr. Ruth Ann Campagna and Rev. Fred Hickok. They have found the sermonettes to be useful and appropriate for worship services, Sunday school, and midweek groups, as well as providing seeds of sermons for adults. I also want to thank Norman Rohrer and Evelyn Minshull for their knowledgeable advice; the Christian Writers' Roundtable, especially Jean W. Sherman, Laurel West, and Emma Westerman, for many hours of inspired critiquing; Sojourners and the Gittings/Loewen ChristCare group from Saint Paul's United Methodist Church, State College, Pennsylvania; and others unnamed who supported this project and me with prayer. In all things, let us remember that "neither the one who plants nor the one who waters is anything, but only God who gives the growth." (1 Corinthians 3:7)

Introduction

Let the words of my mouth and the meditation of my heart be acceptable to you, O Lord, my rock and my redeemer.

—Psalm 19:14

Children are a vital factor in the growth formula of the Christian Church. But attracting four- to eight-year-olds, holding their attention, and teaching them about God can be a daunting task. *Growing Seeds of Faith* is a nondenominational resource to aid pastors and laity who teach children in family worship services. Each lesson is based on a passage of scripture and offers ideas for applying it and sharing faith away from the church.

I pray that the following guidelines and tips will help the seeds of faith that have been planted to grow toward a bountiful harvest.

Guidelines and Tips for *Growing Seeds of Faith*

* Carry props in a bag, basket, box, bucket, or any container appropriate for the topic or the season.
* Gather the children around you at the front of the sanctuary. Sit facing them on their level.
* Tell—don't read—the message. Jot notes on a large index card or copy the lesson pages and keep them on your lap as you talk.
* Read directly from a Bible, bookmarked with sticky notes. All scripture is quoted from the New Revised Standard Version.
* Use a lapel or portable microphone. If children's voices are not amplified, repeat their comments clearly for the congregation.

* Make it fun and interesting. Be loving, but firm, if children become too excited or noisy.
* Use language they understand.
* Pause for children to respond to questions and ideas.
* Expect logical answers from children but remember, also, to expect the unexpected. Be prepared for a few laughs—good medicine for the soul. Parentheses ( ) designate some possible answers. Assure the children when they give good answers.
* Add or substitute your own appropriate experiences or anecdotes. Asterisks (*) mark some opportunities to do this.
* Use the "take-away" to remind children of the lesson. It may be an object or a suggestion of a way to share faith away from the church—learning by doing.
* In children ages four through eight, understanding occurs at different levels. Include "Stretching Further" if more perceptive children need to be challenged. Use it as a part of the basic lesson or in a discussion that continues in a Sunday school class.
* Prayer: Ask the children to bow their heads and repeat your words. Pause between meaningful phrases as children pray aloud.
* Allow five to ten minutes for each lesson. Remember the short attention spans of young children. Adapt the message to their needs and interests. Keep it focused, short, and simple.
* Use most of the messages at any time of the year. See the index for lessons for special days and "holydays."

1
Open Hands

THEME: God wants us to use our hands to show kindness and to do good things.

SCRIPTURE: You open your hand, satisfying the desire of every living thing.—Psalm 145:16

PREPARATION: You may want to use this message on a day when a baby will be baptized or when parents will be present with a young child. Before that day, ask the parents if they would like to participate by joining the children for "message time." Also, plan with the choir director or song leader to sing "Jesus' Hands Were Kind Hands" (*United Methodist Hymnal*, Nashville, Tenn.: United Methodist Publishing House, 1989, 273). If not feasible, read the words as a poem.

I'm thinking about babies today. Does anyone have a new baby sister or brother? Is there a new baby here today? (*As prearranged, invite the parents and child to come forward and join the group of children.*)

Have you ever noticed a new baby's hands? When a baby is born, its hands are closed tightly, like a fist. Let's all close our hands. Then, in a few months, the baby starts to open its hands. Let's open our hands. Some people believe that babies with clenched fists (*close hands*) are holding tightly the blessings, graces, and talents that God gave them. When babies start to open (*open hands*) their hands, they are offering to share those gifts with the world.

We use our hands in many different ways. (*Encourage children to demonstrate ways of communicating with hand signals, or you demonstrate and ask what meaning or feeling results.*) How would you feel if someone did this to you? (*Make a fist in a threatening manner.*) What other ways do we use our hands to show how we feel? (*Have the children use these gestures with one another or with someone in the choir or congregation: shake hands in greeting; wave hello or goodbye; clap; thumbs up; high-five; umpire or referee's signals; traffic signals, and others.)*

Do you think we can find anything about hands in the Bible? Let's look at the book of Psalms. A man named David wrote many of these psalms, and he meant them to be sung. In Psalm 145:16, David praised God by writing, "You open your hand, satisfying the desire of every living thing." God's open hand provides everything we need every day.

In Psalm 139:9 and 10, David praised God by writing, "If I take the wings of the morning and settle at the farthest limits of the sea, even there your hand shall lead me, and your right hand shall hold me fast." God protects us wherever we are and leads us on safe paths.

In still another psalm (31:15), David wrote, "My times are in your hand; deliver me from the hand of my enemies and persecutors." David believed that all of life's happenings were under God's control. God is in charge when we are tiny babies, while we grow, and when we are old. Another writer wrote, "My times are in God's hand, a hand so sure and strong, a hand that holds the seas and guides the stars along."

Those are some of the ways that God uses God's hands; to give us what we need, to protect us, and to be in charge of our lives. How do you think God wants us to use *our* hands? God wants us to use our hands to do good and kind things that make other people feel good. Which do you think God wants you to do: help your brother or sister put a puzzle together or tear the puzzle apart; take and eat the last cookie or share the cookie with someone; write nasty, unkind words or make a beautiful picture; get ready for bed when Mom or Dad says it's time or keep on doing what you're doing?

God wants us to use our hands to help one another, too. Have you ever tried to learn to do something—maybe tying your shoelaces—and someone saw you having a hard time and said, "Let me give you a hand with that"? If someone falls or drops something, how can you give that person a hand? When someone or a group of people does something well, like singing or playing a musical instrument, how can we show them that we appreciate what they have done? Yes, by clapping. We call clapping "giving them a hand," too.

We talked about babies holding their blessings and talents in their hands, and then opening their hands to share the gifts God gave them. You were once a baby with tightly closed hands. But now you can open your hands and share what God has given you.

Here's another way to use your hands. Have you ever had a problem that you felt you couldn't get rid of all by yourself? Maybe someone teases you or takes your lunch money, or maybe you're afraid of thunder and lightning, or a dog that growls at you? What could you do about your problem? Talking about it with your parents is a good idea. Talking to God about it is another good idea. Then after you pray to God for help with what is troubling you, put your hands together to make the shape of a cup or a bowl. *(Demonstrate and ask children to do the same.)* Then imagine that your problem is inside that cup. Then blow it away. Say, "God, it's in your hands now. I know you will help me." And God will.

Optional: Stretching Further

Ask how Jesus used his hands while he lived on earth. *(Washing disciples' feet; putting saliva and his hands on a blind man's eyes to heal him; praying; breaking bread; serving a cup of wine at the Last Supper; blessing the fish to feed a crowd.)* If "Jesus' Hands Were Kind Hands" is familiar, sing it with the children or with the entire congregation. If unfamiliar, read the words as a poem.

Let's pray. *(Ask children to bow their heads and repeat after you. Say short, meaningful phrases.)*

Dear God, thank you for opening your hands to give us everything we need. Thank you for protecting us and being in charge of our lives. Help us to use our hands to do good and kind things, too. Help us to share what you have given us. We pray in Jesus' name. Amen.

2
Be Still!

THEME: Being still (quiet) is an important part of praying.

SCRIPTURE: Be still and know that I am God!—Psalm 46:10

PREPARATION: Obtain headphones to wear and listen (or appear to be listening) to music as the children arrive. Talk with the pastor or liturgist concerning the amount of time that would be feasible for the entire congregation to "be still" along with the children. Obtain or make a party invitation with an RSVP inside and a "thank-you" note.

Oh! Hello! I was so interested in listening to the music (*or radio*) that I almost forgot to come to talk with you! (*Take off headphones.*) You know what these are, don't you? Do you or does someone you know have headphones? Why do people wear headphones?

I've noticed that people jogging along the street often wear headphones. Where else have you seen people wearing headphones?

I've noticed something else, too. There is noise or music almost everywhere I go: in elevators, in stores, at the mall, in cars, in the dentist's office, even in funeral homes. Sometimes the noise bothers me. Sometimes I would just like it to be quiet. When it's noisy all the time, I feel like I can't even hear myself think!

Are there times when *you* don't want to hear anything? You just want a quiet time with no music, no television or radio, no sound of people talking, no noise at all?

Listen to the Word of God in Psalm 46:10 (*read aloud from the Bible*): "Be still and know that I am God!"* When I hear the words "be still," I remember that that's what my mother would say when my brothers and sister and I were being noisy, or arguing, or teasing one another. "Be still!" (*Use a firm, scolding voice.*) She meant that we should stop teasing or arguing and be quiet. But I remember a different way she would say, "be still," too. She might be sitting on a rocking chair, holding a crying baby close to her heart, patting the baby's back, rocking back and forth, and saying gently and softly, "Sh-h-h, be still. Sh-h-h, be still."

How can *you* be still, as the psalmist wrote, and know that God is God? You can start by taking off the headphones and turning off the radio and television and being in a quiet room. If there isn't a quiet spot where you live, maybe you can find a quiet place outside. Or you could turn off the radio and just wear the headphones like earmuffs to help shut out the noise.

Then you need to put aside whatever else you have been thinking about. Clear your mind of all the "noises" inside you. It may not be easy to do, but it's important. Think about God and everything you know about God: God's power, God's love for you, God's being in charge of your life.

Have you ever received an invitation to a party, maybe a birthday party? (*Show the invitation.*) At the bottom of this invitation, it says RSVP. Do you know what RSVP means? Those letters stand for words in the French language—*repondez s'il vous plait*—meaning reply, if you please. It means that the person who invited you wants to know if you will come. The person who is giving the party wants to know how many people to prepare food and drinks for and how many plates, cups, knives, forks, and spoons to have.

When you are still, it's as if you have given God an invitation to come and talk with you. (*Repeat.*) Think about that! God wants to come and talk with you. God accepts your invitation. God says, "Yes, I'll come." When you are still, you are preparing to hear God's voice.

It seems that people have a hard time being still. Have you ever seen someone using a cell phone while shopping in a store or driving a car? Driving that way could be dangerous, because the one who is driving isn't giving all of his or her attention to driving and to the other cars and trucks on the road. Drivers talking on phones can't hear what's going on around them. In the same way, it's almost impossible for us to talk and listen at the same time. Because your teacher knows that, your teacher probably doesn't want you to be talking when you should be listening to directions.

It's like that when we pray, too. If we are busy doing all the talking, we don't hear God's voice. Praying isn't only talking, it's also listening carefully for God's response.

How do you actually hear God? God sometimes speaks to you by giving you thoughts. God speaks through voices. Often God uses conversation with other people whom God has chosen to speak to you. God puts people in your life to bring you closer to God. God uses things that happen to you to let you know God better. Sometimes God speaks to you in dreams, and God speaks to you within your heart.

God speaks to you, not only when you are still and waiting, but also whenever and wherever God wants. In the book of Isaiah (30:15), we read, "In quietness and trust shall be your strength." Even when it's noisy all around you, you can have quietness in your heart because you know that you can trust God to make you strong to face whatever is troubling you.

We need to *learn* to hear God, and we need to keep on learning for the rest of our lives. This week, I hope that each day, maybe just before you go to bed, you will find some quiet time and a quiet place where you can be still and know that God is God. Maybe you could ask your parents if there is a time and place where your whole family could "be still" together!

*After a birthday party for my grandson (*show the invitation again.*), he wrote me a letter (*show letter*) to say "thank you" for coming and for the presents I gave him. Don't forget to say "thank you" to God for talking with you in so many ways.

OPTIONAL: STRETCHING FURTHER
Jesus showed his disciples that even the wind and the stormy seas obeyed his voice when he said, "Peace! Be still!" (*Read aloud Mark 4:35–41.*)

Right now, let's ask everyone here to have a quiet time with us. Let's all bow our heads and be still and let God be God. (*Allow a few minutes, as prearranged.*) Now will everyone repeat after me as we pray aloud? (*Say short, meaningful phrases.*)

Dear God, how great you are! Forgive us for being so busy and so noisy that we forget to listen for your voice. Thank you for loving us. Thank you for talking with us. We pray in Jesus' name. Amen.

3
A Nation under God

THEME: The Lord is my banner.

SCRIPTURE: And Moses built an altar and called it, The Lord is my banner.—Exodus 17:15

PREPARATION: 1. Obtain a flag, banner, or pennant bearing the name or crest of a family or sports team. 2. If a U.S. flag is not displayed in the room where you will meet the children, bring a small flag. Be sure to treat it respectfully.

---

*I brought a flag this morning. (*Show banner with family crest or name.*) I found this flag for sale in Germany in a city called München or Munich. I don't speak much of the German language, and the lady who wanted to sell this banner didn't speak much English. She wondered why I, a visitor, wanted this flag. I pointed to the word "Löwen" on the flag, and then I pointed to myself and said, "Löwen, my name." She told me that Löwen was the name of a champion soccer team. They have been playing and winning soccer games since 1860, the date on the flag. Do you know what kind of animals these are on the corners of the flag? They are lions. Löwen is a German word that means lions. "Löwen-power" means that the team is as strong and ferocious as lions. Sometimes, when my whole family is going to come to my house, I hang out this flag to welcome them and to remind them of our family's heritage.

Where else have you seen banners or flags? In football-game parking lots, people sometimes hang up banners so their friends and family can find them. Have you ever seen the Olympics on television? Hundreds of athletes from countries around the world compete against one another in sports. In the winter Olympics, what kind of sports do you think they might have? (*skiing, ice skating, ice hockey, luge*) What kind of sports might they have in summer? (*swimming, diving, running, basketball, volleyball, baseball, gymnastics*) Before the competition begins, the athletes parade on the track. They follow a leader who holds high their country's flag.

Now let's think back to the time, many years ago, after Moses had led the Israelites out of Egypt. God wanted Moses to organize the people for their journey through the wilderness to the land God had promised them. There were more than six hundred thousand people. Listen to how God wanted them to be organized. (*Read aloud Numbers 2:1–2a.*) The people were told to camp in their tents according to their families and tribes. There were tens of thousands of people in each of the twelve tribes. When they traveled, Judah, the largest tribe, led the way. The people followed their tribe's standard or "ensign," a kind of flag set on a pole for all to see. In that way, each tribe stayed together and its members didn't get lost.

As the Israelites crossed the wilderness, enemies attacked them. These people were called Amalekites, and they wanted to drive the Israelites away from this land that they called their own.

Moses told Joshua to choose some men and go to fight the Amalekites. Joshua did as Moses told him. Then Moses, Aaron, and Hur went to the top of a hill to see the battle. Whenever Moses held his hands above his head toward God (*demonstrate and ask the children to do the same*), the Israelites were winning. It was a sign that the nation of Israel depended on God's power. When Moses' arms got tired, and he lowered them (*demonstrate*), the enemy was winning. Do you know what happened next? Moses sat on a stone with his brother Aaron on one side of him and his friend Hur on the other side. They held up Moses' hands until the Israelites won the battle. (*Ask two children to help you to hold your hands high.*)

Listen to what Moses did after the battle was won. (*Read aloud Exodus 17:15.*) Moses built an altar, a place where they could offer gifts and prayers to God. What did he call the altar? (*"The Lord is my banner."*) Why do you think he gave the altar that name? He could have named the altar "Victory!" He named the altar "The Lord is my banner," because he knew that it is God who gives us the power to defeat the forces of evil. Depending on God is like following the banner of God! When we follow the banner of our Lord, we go where God leads us. We obey God's rules. We follow God's standard, the Bible, so we won't get lost.

Our nation, the United States of America, has a flag, a banner that we carry in parades. Do you know the Pledge of Allegiance—the words that we say to mean that we will be loyal and true to what our nation stands for? In the pledge, we say that the flag stands for "one nation under God." Our faith in God is our greatest strength. Without God, our country cannot live.

OPTIONAL: STRETCHING FURTHER

You can see our country's flag at many places and many times. Where have you seen the American flag? (*At school, perhaps in a parade, a special celebration, in front of someone's house, at sports events.*) How can you show that you respect and honor our flag? When you say the Pledge of Allegiance, you should salute the flag by standing up straight and tall with your right hand over your heart. (*Turn toward the flag and place your right hand over your heart. Ask children to do the same.*) Every time that you see the flag, I hope you will remember that it stands for our country, our "nation under God."

Let's pray. (*Remind children to bow their heads and repeat after you. Say short, meaningful phrases.*)

Dear God, thank you that we can live in this country. Let it be a "nation under God." Help us to follow *your* banner to go where you want us to go in the name of Jesus. Amen.

(*Sing an appropriate song like "America" ("My Country, 'Tis of Thee"). Point out that we sing to "God, author of liberty." We ask God to protect us.*)

4
Gonna Put
On My Shoes

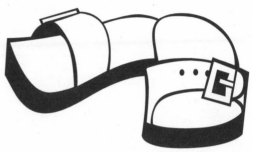

THEME: Shoes can be a sign of God's loving care for us.

SCRIPTURE: I have led you forty years in the wilderness. The clothes on your back have not worn out, and the sandals on your feet have not worn out.—Deuteronomy 29:5

PREPARATION: Wear sandals, if available. This message is especially appropriate for a time, such as the beginning of a new school year, when new shoes are likely to be needed. Be prepared to tell where in the community needy children can obtain free or inexpensive shoes and other articles of clothing.

Today we are going to talk about shoes. *Something funny happened at a picnic I went to a few days ago. A man and woman who sat side by side looked down at their feet and saw that they were wearing shoes that were alike. What seemed even funnier was that their shoes were unusual because they were green and blue and yellow! One person had bought the shoes long ago and the other had bought them a short time ago. People made jokes all evening about the matching shoes.

Are there special times when you are likely to get new shoes? Is anyone wearing new shoes today? What kind of shoes do you like best? What kind of shoes do you think Jesus wore? Does anyone here like to wear sandals? What is a sandal? How is a sandal different from a sneaker?

How long does it take for your feet to get so big that your shoes are too tight? I found something in God's Word—the Bible—about sandals. The people of Israel had been slaves in Egypt until Moses led them out toward the land that God had promised them. But they didn't obey God's laws, and so they were in the wilderness for forty years. Moses reminded the people that God had taken care of them in the desert. This is what God said. (*Read Deuteronomy 29:5.*) Imagine wearing your sandals and your clothes for forty years and not having them wear out!

In another part of the Bible, we read about Jesus sending out the twelve disciples to heal people and to preach about God. (*Read aloud Mark 6:8, 9.*) Did you hear something about sandals? The disciples would be doing a lot of walking. Did you hear what Jesus said they should *not* take with them? (*Read the passage again, if necessary.*) Do you know what a tunic is? (*A straight, shirt-like garment worn under another garment. It had an open neck and no sleeves.*) Why do you think Jesus told his disciples not to take any money, bread, a travel bag, or an extra piece of clothing? Jesus wanted them to start on their journey right away. He didn't want them to spend much time getting ready. Most of all, Jesus wanted them to trust that God would take care of them, just as God had cared for the people of Israel in their forty years in the wilderness.

Does God care for us, too? Maybe there are times when you need something, like new shoes, but you might not be able to get them for a while. How would you feel if you had no shoes?

*Do you know that there is a Shoe Bank in our Sunday school building next door? Children who need new shoes can go there and try on shoes and get a pair without paying any money. A few days ago, I was in a department store, and I saw Mrs. Varner pushing two big carts of brand new sneakers out the door. She was taking those sneakers to the Shoe Bank. Maybe someone in your class at school would like to know about the Shoe Bank. You could tell that person how much you like going to Sunday school. Tell about the fun things you do there and tell about the Shoe Bank. You would be a good friend, and you would be doing good work for God, showing that you care, too. Another way you could help is to give your shoes and boots that are still good but too small for you to the Shoe Bank for someone else to wear.

OPTIONAL: STRETCHING FURTHER

Read or sing with the children a verse of the spiritual that says: "I got shoes, you got shoes; all God's children got shoes. When I get to heaven, gonna put on my shoes, gonna walk all over God's Heaven, Heaven, Heaven. Everybody talkin' about Heaven, ain't goin' there, Heaven, Heaven. Gonna walk all over God's Heaven."

Let's pray. *(Remind children to bow their heads and repeat after you. Say short, meaningful phrases.)*

Dear God, thank you for taking care of us. Thank you for enough food to eat and clothes to wear. Let us be your helpers. Let us be good friends to those who don't have all that they need. We pray in Jesus' name. Amen.

5
Gonna Take Off My Shoes

THEME: We honor God by our attitude and actions.

SCRIPTURE: Then he said, "Come closer! Remove the sandals from your feet, for the place on which you are standing is holy ground."—Exodus 3:5

PREPARATION: Cut two pieces of poster board, about 4 x 11 inches. With a dark, broad-tipped marker, print "attitude" on one card and "action" on the other. Wear sandals, if available, or remove your shoes before greeting the children.

I see that everyone is wearing shoes today. Do you know that in some places people take off their shoes before they go indoors? *Not long ago, a young man from Africa visited me. Before he stepped on the carpet, he took off his shoes. Why do you think he did that?

Do you ever do that at home? *My grandsons take off their shoes when they come to my house. I don't tell them to do that, but their parents tell them, especially if their shoes are very dirty. The floors do stay clean longer that way.

Long ago, people didn't have shoes like the ones that we wear. Do you know what kind of shoes Moses wore? Did Moses wear sneakers? Moses probably wore sandals made from pieces of leather pulled together over the foot with leather thongs or cord. He didn't need to think about which sandal to put on each foot because the right sandal and the left sandal were the same.

There is another reason that people take off their shoes in special places. Listen to this story about Moses. *(Read aloud Exodus 3:1–5.)* What was Moses doing in this story? *(Taking care of a flock of sheep.)* What strange thing did Moses see? *(An angel appeared in a bush that was on fire, but not burning up.)* What did God tell Moses to do? *(Read again Exodus 3:5.)* God told Moses to take off his sandals, because he was standing on holy ground. This ground was set apart for serving and worshiping God.

Moses obeyed God. When he took off his sandals, he showed respect and honor and reverence to God. The people believed that to worship God, they themselves must be clean and wear clean clothes. It wouldn't be proper to wear dirty shoes. Many people today remove their shoes before they go inside a church or temple.

God is our friend, but God is also our Ruler. When we get ready to worship and honor God, do we put on the same clothes we wore to slide in to home plate or splash in a puddle on a rainy day? No, when we come to worship God, we come as though our Ruler has invited us to be a guest.

More important than what we wear is our attitude. *(Show "attitude" card.)* Have you heard that word—"attitude"? Often people today use "attitude" to mean a bad feeling that someone has. Our attitude is how we feel in our minds and hearts about something or someone. The attitude of Christians is that we respect God. We know that God is all-powerful and almighty and all knowing. This awesome God loves and cares for us. Even though most of us don't remove our shoes before we worship God, it's just as important today as it was in Moses' time to show respect and honor to God.

How can we show our attitude toward God? We show our attitude by what we do. Suppose you have been outside playing with your friends, when your mother calls you and says it's time to come in. If you just keep on playing, that means your attitude is that it's not important to obey your mother. If you stop playing, say goodbye to your friends, and go inside, your attitude and what you do—your action *(show "action" card.)*—say that it's important to do what Mom says.

Do you know that when you obey your parents, you are also honoring and obeying God? Have you heard of the Ten Commandments? The Ten Commandments are laws that God gave to Moses for all the people to obey. One of those laws tells us to honor and obey our parents.

Someone asked Jesus, "Which commandment in the law is the greatest?" *(Read aloud Matthew 22:37–39.)* Jesus made the laws seem easier for us to understand and obey. Love God with your whole self and love your neighbor as much as you love yourself.

I hope that every time you take off your shoes, you will remember that you honor God by obeying God's laws. Whom does Jesus say you should love with all your heart, soul, and mind? (*God.*) Whom does Jesus say you should love as much as you love yourself? (*Your neighbor.*)

OPTIONAL: STRETCHING FURTHER

Do you know any more of the Ten Commandments? (*Paraphrase: Don't worship anyone but God. Don't worship an idol. Don't use God's name carelessly. Keep the seventh day as a day of rest. Don't kill or steal or tell lies. Don't even want to take anything that belongs to someone else.*)

Let's pray. (*Remind children to bow their heads and repeat after you. Say short meaningful phrases.*)

Dear God, we want to love you and honor you. Help us to do what you want us to do. Help us to love one another as much as we love ourselves. In Jesus' name. Amen.

6
Puzzling

THEME: Life can be puzzling because we don't always see the whole picture, as God does.

SCRIPTURE: For surely I know the plans I have for you, says the Lord, plans for your welfare and not for harm, to give you a future with hope.—Jeremiah 29:11

PREPARATION: Obtain a sturdy jigsaw puzzle showing a subject of interest to four- to eight-year-olds. Assemble the puzzle but leave out one vital piece. Put that piece in your pocket. If available, obtain an old puzzle to give as "take-away" pieces.

I have a puzzle to show you today. Do you like to put puzzles together? Do you like puzzles that have only a few pieces? Do you like puzzles with lots of pieces? Can you tell what my puzzle shows? What's wrong with my puzzle? (*One piece is missing. Without the missing piece, we can't see the whole picture.*)

Has that ever happened to you? You couldn't finish the puzzle because one piece or more than one piece was missing? Have you ever wanted to play or started to play a game like checkers or a game with cards or marbles and found you couldn't play the game right because a piece was missing? How do you feel when that happens?

I wasn't happy when I found I couldn't finish this puzzle. Sometimes, I think that living is kind of like putting a puzzle together. If I have all the pieces and I put them together in exactly the right way, everything goes well, and I'm happy. But if just one piece isn't in its place, everything turns out differently.

Here's what I mean. Pretend it's morning at your house on a school day. You get dressed, eat your favorite breakfast, brush your teeth, take your lunch or lunch money and your backpack, and go wait for the bus. The bus is exactly on time, and you sit with your best friend. When you walk into your classroom, there's your teacher at the desk, ready to start the day's lessons. Everything is going well. It's like having all the pieces of the puzzle and putting each one in just the right place.

Have you ever had a day that started out differently? Maybe someone else ate the last of your favorite cereal or used the last bit of toothpaste, or the bus was late and someone else was sitting beside your best friend. Maybe when you walked into your classroom, there was a new teacher sitting at your teacher's desk. That kind of day feels like the pieces of the puzzle aren't fitting together in the right way, or a piece of the puzzle is missing.

*I heard today that many people died in a plane crash. Those people are fathers, mothers, grandparents, brothers, sisters, sons, and daughters to someone. For their families, it's not a day when everything goes on as usual. Some parts of the puzzle are missing, and they may always be missing. It's a sad day, and I am sad for those families.

But there is one who sees the whole picture, even if pieces are missing. This is what God told Jeremiah to tell the people. (*Read Jeremiah 29:11.*) God is good, and God has good plans for us. God doesn't plan to hurt us. When bad, sad things happen, God can bring something good from it. God knows the future and goes with us as we do what God wants us to do. God wants to help us through hard times.

(*Reach into your pocket.*) "Oh! Look what I found! Here's the missing piece of my puzzle! I had it all along." (*Complete the puzzle.*)

I have some extra puzzle pieces from an old puzzle. I'm going to give each of you a piece of the puzzle to carry in your pocket. When you are puzzled and don't understand why something sad or bad has happened, let this puzzle piece remind you that God sees the whole picture. In God's plans, good things happen, and God is ready to help you. Maybe you can't see anything good happening right now, but some day you can look back and see how God brought a blessing from unhappy times. That blessing will be much better than you can even imagine.

OPTIONAL: STRETCHING FURTHER

Listen to what the apostle Paul wrote in a letter to the Christians in a city called Rome. *(Read Romans 8:28.)* Paul meant that everything that happens to us will be used for some good. God promises to fit everything together to make a beautiful picture out of our lives. God makes that promise to everyone who loves God.

Let's pray. *(Remind children to bow their heads and repeat after you. Say short, meaningful phrases.)*

Dear God, thank you for loving us. Thank you for the good plans you have for us. We know that you are always ready to help us. We pray in Jesus' name. Amen.

7

Watermelon Wisdom

THEME: From God's creation we can learn about God.

SCRIPTURE: O Lord, how manifold are your works! In wisdom you have made them all; the earth is full of your creatures.
—Psalm 104:24

PREPARATION: 1. Plan with the choir director or song leader to sing "All Things Bright and Beautiful" from *The United Methodist Hymnal* (Nashville, Tenn.: United Methodist Publishing House, 1989), 147, after the prayer. 2. If available, obtain a watermelon or a part of one. Remove the seeds. Rinse and dry enough seeds to tape one seed per child on an index card.

I had a silly thought on my way to church today. Do you ever think silly things? This is what I was thinking: When it rains, what if it rained noodles instead of rain? Isn't that silly? I had some more silly ideas: What if, instead of the sun, there was a big shoe in the sky? What if people had two long legs and two short legs like a kangaroo? That's really silly!

Let's play a game. I'm going to give you an idea. You think about it. If you think it's a silly idea, say, "Silly." If you think it's really true, say, "True." Here's the first idea:

1. Our brains are in our toes. (*Silly.*) Where are our brains?
2. A child is the boss in the family. (*Silly.*) In Ephesians 6:1 we read, "*Children, obey your parents,*" not "Parents, obey your children."
3. From the things that God made, we can learn about God. (*True.*) Listen to what the writer of Psalm 104 says. (*Read aloud Psalm 104:24.*) God made many things. God wasn't silly when God

created the universe and everything in it. God was wise in making everything.

4. Here's another idea. Is it silly or true? Watermelons grow on trees. (*Silly.*) What could happen if you sat under a watermelon tree? Where do watermelons grow? (*On vines on the ground.*) Do you think God was wise to have watermelons grow on the ground instead of on trees? Why? (Watermelons can weigh five to one hundred pounds!)

Let's see how wise God was in making watermelons. If someone had never seen a watermelon, how would you tell that person what it looks like? Do you like to eat watermelon? How does it taste? What happens when you pick up a slice and bite into it? Do you know that almost all of the watermelon is water? If we imagine the watermelon as being made of one hundred parts of what God used to create it, ninety-three of those one hundred parts are water. Maybe that's why it tastes so good on a hot day. What protects that sweet, juicy, delicious part inside it?

What shape is the watermelon? (*Round or oblong.*) Have you ever seen watermelons growing in a field? Because the melons are round or oblong, a strong wind could send them rolling away, getting bruised or broken. God was wise in having the watermelon grow on a vine with long, trailing stems called "runners." These runners can grow as long as forty feet. (*Compare with a measure of your surroundings.*) The long runners then grow thin stems that wind around something in the field, maybe a corn stalk, to hold on to so the wind can't send the melon rolling away.

Suppose all of the watermelons have been eaten and there are no more watermelons anywhere. We would be very sad if that happened. But God gave watermelons seeds to grow more watermelons. The seeds will grow roots and vines with runners. God sends sunshine and rain to help them to grow and make more watermelons. What a wise plan! When we eat watermelon, it gives us vitamins that we need to grow, too.

Watermelons are only one small part of the universe that God has made. We know that God made all things. In the first chapter of the first book in the Bible, we can read about God's creation. (*Read aloud Genesis 1:31a.*)

Do you think God is wise even now? Was God wise yesterday? Will God be wise tomorrow? Is God wise all the time? I say, "God is wise," and then you say, "all the time." Let's try it. (*Ask the congrega-*

tion to participate if you wish.) Now I say, "All the time," and you say, "God is wise."

We have talked mostly about only one thing that God made. We have talked only about how wise God is. From what God has created, we can learn many things about God. But for today, let's remember that God is wise all the time.

OPTIONAL: STRETCHING FURTHER
God loves to give good things to us. Can you think of other good gifts God has given us? (*Perhaps a variety of foods, families, a place to love, clothing, friends, pets, freedom.*)

Let's pray now. (*Ask children to bow their heads and repeat after you.*)

Dear God, you are so wise and good and kind. Thank you for watermelons. Thank you for all the things you have made. Help us to learn more about you. Help us to be more like you. We pray in Jesus' name. Amen.

Here is something to help you to remember that God is wise all the time. It's a watermelon seed. (*Hand out watermelon seed cards.*) God didn't make watermelons to grow on trees. God's way is always wise. God's way is always best. (*If time permits, sing "All Things Bright and Beautiful."*)

8
Plug In! I'm Ready!

THEME: God is all-powerful and always ready to help us.

SCRIPTURE: Have you not known? Have you not heard? The Lord is the everlasting God, the Creator of the ends of the earth. He does not faint or grow weary; his understanding is unsearchable. He gives power to the faint, and strengthens the powerless.
—Isaiah 40:28–29

PREPARATION: 1. Obtain something (a toy, small radio, tape or CD player, microphone, hair dryer, toaster, electric razor) that requires batteries or electricity to function. Prepare to demonstrate the item without plugging it in, and with its source of power. 2. Bookmark selected scripture passages. 3. Search the Internet for "Reddy Kilowatt." You may want to print his likeness or make a poster-size drawing to show to the children.

(As though out of breath from hurrying) I'm a little bit late this morning. Excuse me. I need to catch my breath. I'm late because I had to wait for my hair to dry. I washed it this morning and, of all times, today my hair dryer didn't work! I wonder what's wrong with it. See? *(Demonstrate trying to use the dryer without plugging it into an outlet.)* It doesn't work! Do you have any idea why it doesn't work? *(Anticipate a child's noticing that the electrical cord isn't plugged in. If there is an outlet nearby, plug in the appliance to show that it works.)* Oh, I'm so embarrassed! I've been awfully forgetful lately. But how could I forget to plug the hair dryer into the outlet? Next time I won't forget. That's for sure!

Lots of things need to be plugged in to electricity in order to work. What else needs electricity? *(Vacuum cleaner, coffee maker, mixer,* blender, washer, dryer, power tools, microphone, television, toaster, computer, air conditioner, fan, heater.) Electricity has the power to make all these things work.

There are things in nature that have power, too. I'm thinking of a flood. Floodwaters have power to move and upset things like cars and houses and barns. What else in nature has a lot of power? (Sun, wind, hurricane, tornado, ocean tide, fire, volcano.)

What is the most powerful thing you can think of? Is God as powerful as that? God is more powerful than that! The Word of God— the Bible—tells us about God's power. Listen to what God's Word says about how powerful God is. (Read aloud Jeremiah 51:15–16.) What did you hear about God's power? God is so powerful that God . . . (reread scripture as needed to encourage children to answer) . . . made the earth; established the world; stretched out the heavens; makes lightning, rain, and wind.

In Psalm 147:4 we read, "Great is our Lord, and abundant in power; his understanding is beyond measure." God's power is so great that we can't measure it; we can't describe it or understand it. We say that God is omnipotent; that means God is all-powerful. God is almighty. We can't even imagine how great Almighty God's power is!

Listen to what a prophet named Isaiah wrote about God. (Read aloud Isaiah 40:28–29.) God promises to give power to those who are weak or tired. God promises to give power to those who have no power. Even strong people get tired sometimes. Does God get tired? No. God is never too tired or too busy to help and listen. Even though God gives power away, God doesn't get weak or have less power. God never loses power. After giving strength away, God is as strong as before. God is so strong that God makes us as strong as we need to be to do what God wants us to do.

Jesus is our power source. He is our connection to God, and we need to make sure that we are plugged in. A long time ago, when companies became able to provide electricity for everyone to use, they used newspaper ads showing a little character named Reddy Kilowatt. (Show picture, if available.) Reddy had a body that looked like a lightning bolt. His nose was a light bulb. His ears looked like electrical outlets. Reddy was saying, "Plug in! I'm Reddy!" Reddy wanted people to know that all they had to do was to plug the end of the electrical cord into the outlet—the connection—on the wall. Instantly, they would have electrical power to use.

An electrical-power company still uses Reddy Kilowatt as their symbol for electricity.

We still plug into outlets to get electricity, but please don't you do that without your parents saying that it's okay. You could get hurt if you put anything else into an outlet, too. Please don't play with electricity. It's powerful when we use it as we should, but it's dangerous if we are careless.

Have you noticed that sometimes the lights get dim? During a storm, the electric lights might go off altogether. Why do you think that happens? Something has broken the connection of the electricity flowing from the power station through the wires to the lights. It could be several hours before the connection is fixed so that we can have electricity again.

When my hair dryer wasn't plugged in, it didn't work, did it? When we forget to stay connected to Jesus, sometimes we aren't kind and we do things that are wrong. How can we "plug in" to Jesus? We can pray. We can be sorry for the wrongs we have done. We can learn about Jesus and God in the Bible. We can spend time with other people who believe in Jesus. We can love and obey God, and we can love one another. Doing these things helps us to "plug in" and stay connected to Jesus. Jesus loves us so much that he is always ready to be our power source. We can be sure of that.

Today and all through the week, you will probably use lots of things that need electricity to work. When you turn on the lights, or use a toaster, a radio, a television set, or something else that uses electrical power, let that remind you that God is all-powerful. Before you turn out the lights and go to sleep, remember to connect again with Jesus and say another prayer. God watches over you when you are awake and when you sleep.

OPTIONAL: STRETCHING FURTHER

Read additional selections of scripture. After each reading, have children finish your sentence: God is so powerful that . . .

1. Psalm 147:4: God counts the stars and names each one.
2. Luke 11:20: God, through Jesus Christ, performed miracles.
3. 1 Corinthians 6:14: God brought Jesus from death to life.
4. Ephesians 1:20–22: God is in control of everything.

Let's pray now. Please bow your heads and repeat after me. (*Say short, meaningful phrases.*)

Almighty God, you are all-powerful. We can't imagine how powerful you are! Thank you for sending Jesus to connect us to you. Help us to remember that you give us the power to do what you want us to do. We pray in Jesus' name. Amen.

9
Running Away

THEME: God is present everywhere and nothing can separate us from God's love.

SCRIPTURE: For I am convinced that neither death, nor life, nor angels, nor rulers, nor things present, nor things to come, nor powers, nor height, nor depth, nor anything else in all creation, will be able to separate us from the love of God in Christ Jesus our Lord.—Romans 8:38–39

PREPARATION: Obtain *The Runaway Bunny*, a classic picture book by Margaret Wise Brown. Prepare to read it aloud or tell the story while showing the illustrations to the children.

I'm going to read (*or tell*) you a story about a rabbit—a bunny. The bunny in this story can talk and do lots of other things that real rabbits can't do. It's a make-believe story—a pretend story. Will you pretend with me?

This little bunny was unhappy. We don't know exactly why he was unhappy. What makes you unhappy? Maybe he didn't like to make his bed, put his toys away, keep his room neat, take out the garbage, or go to school. (*If book is available, show illustrations while you read.*) He was so unhappy that he said to his mother, "I'm running away!"

His mother said, "If you run away, I will run after you. You are my little bunny."

Little Bunny said, "If you run after me, I will become a fish in a stream and I'll swim away from you."

"If you become a fish, I will become a fisherman and I will fish for you," said Mother Bunny.

Little Bunny said, "If you become a fisherman, I will become a rock on a high mountain."

What do you think his mother said? "I'll be a mountain climber. I'll climb to where you are."

So Little Bunny goes on saying what he will become when he runs away. What does his mother go on saying? She will become something or someone who will find him. (*Continue telling what Little Bunny says he will become and encourage children to guess what Mother will do.*) When Little Bunny says he will become a flower in a garden, what do you think his mother will become? (*A gardener.*) When Little Bunny says he will be a bird and fly away, what will Mother be? (*A tree that Little Bunny comes home to.*) Bunny will become a sailboat and sail away. What will Mother become? (*The wind and blow him where she wants him to go.*) Little Bunny will join a circus and fly away on a flying trapeze. What will Mother be? (*A tightrope walker and walk across to him.*)

At last Little Bunny says, "If you become a tightrope walker and walk across the air, I will become a little boy and run into a house."

Mother Bunny says, "I will become your mother and catch you in my arms and hug you."

"Shucks, " says Little Bunny, "I might as well stay where I am and be your little bunny."

And so he did.

"Have a carrot," said Mother Bunny.

How do you think Little Bunny feels at the end of the story? Why? Did Mother Bunny love Little Bunny? No matter what he became or where he went, she did what she needed to do to find him. She kept on loving him.

This story is called *The Runaway Bunny*. It was written a long time ago by Margaret Wise Brown. Would you believe that my friend Julie found a story in the Bible that is very much like *The Runaway Bunny*?

Listen while I read what David says to God. (*Read aloud Psalm 139:7–10.*) David says I can't flee—run away—from God. Wherever I go, God is there, leading me, holding me by the hand. God loves me. Little Bunny really couldn't run away from his mother, either, could he?

In another part of the Bible, we can read a letter that the apostle Paul wrote to the Christians in Rome. (*Read aloud Romans 8:38, 39.*) Paul says that nothing—troubles, problems, danger, death, nothing above us or below us, nothing now or in the future, nothing else in the whole world—can separate us from God's love.

Wherever we are, there God is, too. There are no limits to God's love. No fence or door or wall, no ocean or mountain or storm can keep God away from us. Even if we wanted to escape from God, we couldn't do it.

If you ever get angry and feel like running away from what makes you angry or terribly unhappy, I hope you will remember the runaway bunny. Remember that God loves you even more than Mother Bunny loves her little one.

OPTIONAL: STRETCHING FURTHER

Listen to what David says about darkness. *(Read Psalm 139:10–12.)* David says that even when it's dark, to God, the night is as bright as day. Have you ever been afraid of the dark? God says you don't need to be afraid.

Let's pray. *(Remind children to bow their heads and repeat after you. Say short, meaningful phrases.)*

Dear God, we are glad that you are always with us. Thank you for loving us so much. We pray in Jesus' name. Amen.

10
How Precious!

THEME: We are God's precious children.

SCRIPTURE: People were bringing little children to him in order that he might touch them; and the disciples spoke sternly to them. But when Jesus saw this, he was indignant and said to them, "Let the little children come to me; do not stop them; for it is to such as these that the kingdom of God belongs. Truly, I tell you, whoever does not receive the kingdom of God as a little child will never enter it." And he took them in his arms, laid his hands on them, and blessed them.—Mark 10:13–16

PREPARATION: Bring a stuffed animal, doll, or blanket, preferably well worn, that might be precious (much loved, dear) to a child.

---

*I have a friend who has a new baby. Do any of you have a new baby sister or brother or cousin? Is there a baby in your building or neighborhood? How do grown-ups act around new babies? Have you noticed? Do they act as if they like new babies?

I was talking to my friend whose baby is a few months old. We talked about when the baby sleeps, how her Daddy likes to give her a bath, and the happy little noises she makes. My friend said, "She is so precious!" What do you think she meant when she said that her baby is precious? (*The baby is loved a lot.*)

Let's think about what is precious to you. Are there people who are precious to you?

Does anyone have something that you like to take with you, especially if you're going away overnight? A favorite stuffed animal or teddy bear? Do you like to sleep with your favorite stuffed animal? Do you have a favorite blanket? Do you remember when you did have a favorite blanket or stuffed animal?

Have you seen Charlie Brown on a TV show or in a comic strip? Charlie's friend, Linus, carries his precious blanket with him everywhere he goes. *My son had a favorite light-blue blanket that he liked to take with him. He liked to chew on a corner of it. I washed it so many times that it wore out and came apart. Finally all that was left of it was one little piece. So my son carried that little corner of it in his jacket pocket. He loved that blanket; it was precious to him.

What do you think is precious to Jesus? When Jesus was a baby or a little boy, do you think he had a favorite blanket or a teddy bear? Listen to these words from the Bible. (Read aloud Mark 10:13–16.) Did you hear about something that is precious to Jesus? People brought little children to him, but Jesus' disciples didn't think that parents should bother Jesus with their children. Then Jesus said, "Let them come to me." He touched them and blessed them because little children are precious to Jesus.

What about big children? Are they precious to Jesus, too? You were once a precious baby, but has anyone called you precious lately? Sometimes parents forget to tell their big children how precious they are, just as precious as they were when they were babies.

What about grown-ups? Are they precious to Jesus, too? Jesus said that whoever believes in God as little children do is precious to God. Big children and grown-ups must simply trust God and believe in Jesus as little children do.

The Bible tells us how much God loves us. (Read aloud 1 John 3:1a.) God loves all of us like precious children, and that is what we are—children of God. We belong to God.

Jesus tells us in another way how precious we are. (Read aloud Matthew 10:29–31.) Jesus said that God knows how many hairs are on your head. God knows what happens even to one sparrow. You are far more valuable to God than a whole flock of sparrows. You are so precious that God sent you Jesus—God's precious child.

This week, when you go to bed with your favorite blanket or play with your favorite stuffed animal, remember how precious you are to God. You are so precious that you can take Jesus with you, in your heart, everywhere you go.

OPTIONAL: STRETCHING FURTHER
Talk about Jesus. Why is he our most precious possession? (*Jesus is our friend and Savior.*)

Let's pray. (*Remind children to bow their heads and repeat after you. Say short, meaningful phrases.*)

Dear God, thank you for loving us. We know that we are precious to you. Thank you for Jesus, your precious gift to us. Help us to remember that Jesus is with us wherever we go. We pray in Jesus' name. Amen.

11
God's Temple

THEME: Your body is God's temple. Take good care of it.

SCRIPTURE: Do you not know that your body is a temple of the Holy Spirit within you, which you have from God, and that you are not your own?—1 Corinthians 6:19

PREPARATION: From two different colors of poster board, index cards, or sticky note paper, cut enough square-inch pieces to give one of each color to each child. On one set of squares, write the number "1"; on the other set, write the number "2." You will also need to bring a ruler.

Today, we are going to talk about you and your amazing body. Look at your skin. How much do you think your skin will weigh when you become a grown-up? The answer is about six pounds.

Here is a piece of paper that measures one square inch. (*Show with a ruler that it measures one inch on each side. Then place the paper square on the back of your hand.*) This square inch of paper is covering one square inch of my skin. That square inch of skin has in it nineteen million cells, sixty hairs, ninety oil glands, nineteen feet of blood vessels, six hundred twenty-five sweat glands, and nineteen thousand sensory cells that let us feel hot and cold and rough and smooth. Isn't that amazing?

We can learn many things about our bodies. Who made our bodies? God created Adam and Eve, the first people. God formed their bodies. In Psalm 139, David sings to the Lord. (*Read aloud Psalm 139:14a.*) You are wonderfully made, too.

The apostle Paul wrote about your body in a letter to the people at Corinth. (*Read aloud 1 Corinthians 6:19.*) What did Paul say about your body? (*Read the passage again.*) Your body is a temple. What's a temple? A temple is a building where people worship God, just as this church is where we worship God.

King Solomon had the first temple to God built almost a thousand years before Jesus was born. It was beautiful! It was built of white limestone on a hill in Jerusalem. The wooden doors had carvings of palm trees and flowers and angels with gold wings. Inside the temple were more angels, ten golden candleholders, and a golden table for twelve loaves of bread. In a special place, the tablets of stone that held the Ten Commandments were kept.

The Hebrew people believed that God was always in the temple, just as God is here in this church building. How do you think the people felt about the temple? Listen to what the writer of Psalm 84 says. *(Read aloud Psalm 84:1 and 84:4.)* Were they happy with the temple? They were so happy and full of joy that they felt like singing.

Paul said your body is a temple with God's Spirit inside. How does it make you feel to know that your body is like God's beautiful temple? I hope it makes you feel good about the body God has given you.

Now think about where you live. If your family rents your home, the owner probably has rules you need to obey to keep it safe and clean. Maybe you aren't allowed to leave toys in the hallway or bring pets indoors.

Do your parents have rules, too, such as these: Don't draw on the walls; take off your shoes before you come inside; bat the ball away from the house?

Paul wrote that you are not your own. You belong to God. What rules do you need to obey to keep your body a safe, clean, beautiful place for God to live? Let's find out. I'm going to give each of you two "square inches." One square has the number "1" on it. The other has the number "2." I'm going to read two things that you can do. One thing will be a better way for you to make your body strong and healthy. Listen while I read them. Then decide: Is the first way better, or is the second way better? If the first is better, hold up square 1; if the second way is better, hold up square 2. Let's try it.

A. 1.) Wash your hands with soap and water before you eat. 2.) After you are done playing outside, go straight to the cookie jar and get a cookie. Which is better? Number one or number two? Number one is better. Who knows why it's better to wash your hands before you eat?

B. 1.) On a hot day, drink a lot of soft drinks. 2.) On a hot day, drink water often. *(2 is better.)*

C. 1.) Eat chips and cookies for a snack. 2.) Eat an apple or carrot sticks for a snack. (*2 is better.*)

D. 1.) Run across the street as fast as you can. 2.) Look carefully both ways before you walk across the street. (*2 is better.*)

E. 1.) Watch cartoons on television. 2.) Shoot hoops or baskets. (*2 is better.*)

F. 1.) Go to bed when Dad or Mom says that it's time. 2.) Stay up and awake until you can't keep your eyes open any longer. (*1 is better.*)

When we take good care of ourselves, we are giving our best to God.

I want you to take the two "square inches" with you. Carry them in your pocket to remind you that you are God's temple. Keep God's temple clean and safe and strong every day.

OPTIONAL: STRETCHING FURTHER

These are some ways that you can take good care of God's temple: Eat foods that build strong muscles and bones. Drink water, orange juice, and milk. Get some exercise every day. Get enough sleep. Obey safety rules. Can you think of other ways? (*Wear a seat belt. Wear a helmet to ride a bicycle or a scooter or play baseball, soccer, or football. Don't play with matches. Don't get into a car with a stranger. Don't put anything into your mouth that isn't good for you. Don't go into a pool alone.*)

Let's pray. (*Ask children to bow their heads and repeat after you. Say short, meaningful phrases.*)

Dear God, thank you for our amazing bodies. Help us to follow your rules for keeping your temple beautiful, safe, and strong. We pray in Jesus' name. Amen.

12
A Mighty Mite

THEME: A small gift can accomplish great things for God's work.

SCRIPTURE: He sat down opposite the treasury, and watched the crowd putting money into the treasury. Many rich people put in large sums. A poor widow came and put in two small copper coins, which are worth a penny. Then he called his disciples and said to them, "Truly I tell you, this poor widow has put in more than all those who are contributing to the treasury. For all of them have contributed out of their abundance; but she out of her poverty has put in everything she had, all she had to live on."—Mark 12:41–44

PREPARATION: 1. Identify a specific project that can be supported by children's offerings. 2. Obtain enough pennies to give ten to each child. You may want to put them in small envelopes. 3. On an 8" x 11" piece of cardboard, mount a penny, nickel, dime, and quarter with small pieces of mailing tape, rolled to make double-sided sticky surfaces. 4. Investigate local stores, theaters, or malls to see what, if anything, can be bought for a penny, nickel, dime, or quarter. 5. For "Stretching Further," make three poster board word cards, each about 4" x 11". With a dark, broad marker, print one word on each card: "mite," "might," and "mighty."

I brought some money today. (*Show display board.*) Who knows what we call this coin? (*Indicate the penny. Then ask the names of the nickel, dime, and quarter.*) If you could have one of these coins, which one would you choose? Why? What could you do with that coin? What could you buy with it? (*Ask what the children could do with each coin. Make suggestions, if necessary.*)

Do you know a Bible story about money? I'm going to read what Jesus told his disciples about money. But first, there are some words you need to know. One word is "treasury." Jesus sat in a part of the temple where he could see people putting money into the treasury. The treasury was a money box or collection box where people could put their offerings. Jesus saw a widow there. A "widow" is a woman whose husband has died. Jesus talked about the widow's poverty. "Poverty" means being poor. So you will know that the woman was a poor widow. *(Read aloud Mark 12:41–44.)*

What had Jesus seen the rich people do? What had he seen the woman do? What did Jesus tell his disciples about the woman? Why did Jesus say that the poor woman had given more than the rich people had given? Jesus knew that the rich people had plenty of everything they needed. They gave only what they didn't need for themselves. The poor woman needed her small coins to live on. Perhaps she could have kept one of those two tiny coins to buy food for herself, but she gave both coins, all that she had. So Jesus said that the poor widow's gift, even though it was small, was more than the rich people's gifts.

*Not long ago, I visited Ukraine, a faraway country where my husband's family had lived. The people in the village were poor. They were happy to see us and wanted to thank us for coming to see them. Just before we left, a woman came walking from the far end of the village. She had brought us a small bunch of sweet red grapes. It was a small gift, but it meant a lot to us. She gave the grapes to us because it was fruit from the land where my husband's family had lived. It was all she had to give, but it was a gift of love, and she gave it cheerfully.

Long ago, God gave Moses some laws about giving to God. *(Read aloud Deuteronomy 14:22–23.)* Moses told the people that God wanted them to "tithe"—to give one part out of every ten parts of what they had harvested in the fields and the first sheep, goats, and cattle born among their animals. God's people should use part of their tithe to help to feed others who couldn't help themselves, those who were hungry and poor. God would bless the givers in all of their work. When we obey God's laws about giving to those who need help, we are sharing God's goodness to us. Giving cheerfully is a way to show others what God is like.

Do you think it is easy or hard to tithe, to give one part out of ten? If you have ten pennies, how many pennies would be a tithe? If you have ten dollars? If you have one hundred dollars? Sometimes, when people have a lot of money, it can be hard for them to give a tithe to help others and to do God's work. But if you start tithing when you are young, it may be easier to keep on giving a tithe as you grow older.

I brought a lot of pennies today. If I gave each of you ten pennies, what would you do with the ten cents? Would you want to give all ten pennies to help people who need food or clothes or a warm place to sleep? (*Name a current project, if feasible.*) Would you want to give five pennies to help them? Would you want to give one penny, a tithe? Would you want to save the pennies?

(*Give each child an envelope containing ten pennies.*) When you go to your classroom or when the ushers pass the offering plate, you will have a chance to give an offering. It's up to you. You decide if you want to give any of these ten pennies today. You may think that your one penny can't buy anything to help anyone. But if a lot of people give one penny, together the pennies will add up to a bigger offering that can help someone who needs it. Remember that God loves it when you are happy to give and share what you have.

OPTIONAL: STRETCHING FURTHER

Sometimes, in the story of the poor widow's offering, we use the word "mite" instead of coins. A mite is a very small thing or a very small coin. The widow's offering was very small, a mite (*Show "mite" word card.*), but Jesus said she gave more than the rich people gave. There's another way that we use a word that sounds like mite, but we spell it with different letters, like this. (*Show "might" word card.*) This word, "might," means having great power or strength. If we put another letter, "Y," on the end of it (*show word card that says "mighty"*), it says "mighty." We know that God is almighty. God has awesome power and strength. To God, the widow's coins were a treasure. Her little bit became a lot. It was a mighty offering. Many years later, her story still teaches us about giving.

Let's pray. (*Remind children to bow their heads and repeat after you. Say short, meaningful phrases.*)

Dear God, thank you for showing us how to give and share what you give to us. Help us to remember that you can do mighty things with our small gifts. We pray in Jesus' name. Amen.

13
The Words of My Mouth

THEME: The words we say should please God.

SCRIPTURE: Let the words of my mouth and the meditation of my heart be acceptable to you, O Lord, my rock and my redeemer—Psalm 19:14

PREPARATION: 1. Gather an assortment of word games and activities, such as Scrabble, an easy crossword puzzle, and an easy word search. 2. Make enough copies of the word search at the end of this message to give one to each child. 3. You may want to use the beautiful song, "Psalm 19," by Terry Butler from *Touching the Father's Heart: Before You Now Songbook* (Anaheim, Calif.: Mercy/Vineyard, 1994), words 102, accompaniment 88.

Today we are going to talk about talking. What we are really going to talk about is words. Is there anyone here who has not yet said a word today? Have you said "Good morning"? Let's all say "Good morning" together. (*If children don't respond heartily, encourage them to try again.*) Do you know what it means when you say "Good morning" to someone? "Good morning" means "I hope you have a good morning. I hope everything that happens makes you happy."

Think about the words you have already spoken today. Did you need to tell someone what you wanted to eat? Did you need to ask which clothes you should wear? Did you say "please" or "thank you" to anyone? How many words do you think you have already said today?

Words are important, aren't they? It would be very hard to get along without them. When you were a baby, though, you had another way to let your parents know that you were hungry or sleepy.

What did you do? When you were happy, you smiled and giggled.

Now that you have learned to use words, you can do fun things with them, too. Do you know any games you can play with words? (*Scrabble®, Upwords, Password™, Boggle, computer games.*) Have you ever done a crossword puzzle or a word search? (*Show word games and activities.*) Another fun thing to do is finding words that you can read forward and backward. One word like that is dog, "d—o—g." Spelled backward, it says "g—o—d," god. A number that is the same forward and backward is 2002.

Where can we find a lot of printed words? (*In church bulletins, hymnals, newspapers, magazines, the Internet.*) If I want to know what a word means, where should I look? (*Dictionary.*) If I want to learn about God, where should I look? (*Bible.*) If I want to know what Jesus said, where should I look?

We can find thousands of words in the Bible. Among all those words, I found a song that a man named David wrote to praise God. David wrote this song hundreds of years before the baby Jesus was born. (*Read aloud Psalm 19:14.*) Have you heard a song with those words that David wrote? Sometimes, we say, "pleasing" instead of "acceptable." David hoped that his words would please God. He hoped that even his thoughts—what he was thinking about but didn't say out loud—would please God.

What kinds of words do you think God likes to hear? Do you think God likes to hear, "Thank you"? Kind words or unkind words? Gentle words or harsh words? Lying words or honest words? Wrong words or right words? Words that help people to get along with one another or words that start quarrels?

David knew that God not only heard the words that he said, but God also knew his thoughts, the meditation of his heart. David wanted his thoughts to please God, too. We show what is in our hearts by the kinds of words we use.

Words are powerful. We can use words that will make someone angry or happy. Words can confuse or explain and teach. Words can say evil things or remind someone that God is good. Words can help or hurt. Words can cause fights or settle arguments.

God is always pleased with words that keep us moving in God's direction and bring glory to Jesus. When we say the names of God and Jesus, we should say them in a way that shows that we love and honor and respect God and God's child. God is not pleased when we use those names carelessly.

OPTIONAL: STRETCHING FURTHER
David, at the end of his song, Psalm 19:14, calls God "Lord, my rock and my redeemer." Why do you think David thinks of God as a rock? (*A large rock is strong and a good place to hide. God is strong and protects us from our enemies.*) Sometimes God is compared to a rocky mountain where God's people can run for safety and shelter. (*Read aloud Psalm 18:1–2.*)

Let's pray now. Please bow your heads. Repeat after me. (*Say short phrases.*)

Dear God, let the words of my mouth and the meditation of my heart be pleasing to you, O Lord. Let your love guide our thoughts and our words. We pray in Jesus' name. Amen.

David's song is really a prayer. It's a prayer that we can pray every day. I am going to give you a reminder of that prayer. (*Distribute word search activity sheets.*) Maybe a brother, a sister, or parent might help you to find the hidden words. Keep practicing David's prayer every day. Next week let's all say it together.

			P			L	O	R	D	
			L		B	E	F			W
		M	E	D	I	T	A	T	I	O	N
M	T	O	A	N	D		H	E	A	R	T
Y	O	U	S						D	H
		T	I						S	E
		H	N						
			G						

(KEY)

David's Prayer

Q	R	Z	P	U	K	L	O	R	D	B	D
F	D	W	L	V	B	E	F	Y	P	W	O
G	L	M	E	D	I	T	A	T	I	O	N
M	T	O	A	N	D	Q	H	E	A	R	T
Y	O	U	S	C	H	E	B	X	J	D	H
S	E	T	I	A	R	E	S	Z	H	S	E
W	M	H	N	Q	L	F	K	Y	O	U	A
U	Y	F	G	V	A	T	N	M	L	I	S

Find these words in the box. Letters may be found in left to right rows or top to bottom columns. Draw a ring around each word.

LET THE WORDS OF MY MOUTH AND MEDITATION
HEART BE PLEASING TO YOU O LORD

Let David's prayer be your prayer every day.

14
A Holy Mystery

THEME: We don't need to understand the mystery of the gospel. We only need to believe.

SCRIPTURE: I became its [the church's] servant according to God's commission that was given to me for you, to make the word of God fully known, the mystery that has been hidden throughout the ages and generations but has now been revealed to his saints. To them God chose to make known how great among the Gentiles are the riches of the glory of this mystery, which is Christ in you, the hope of glory.—Colossians 1:25–27

PREPARATION: Obtain a puzzle that you can solve but will be difficult for the children to solve immediately. An alternative might be for you to tell about a real mystery that took a long time to solve.

I brought something to show you today. *(Show puzzle box.)* This is a puzzle box that my brother sent to me a long time ago. He was in Hawaii and he sent it to me at Christmastime. When I give it to you for a closer look, you will see that the outside has patterns and pictures made with many tiny pieces of wood of different colors. This box is called a Japanese puzzle box. Can you guess why it's called a puzzle box? There doesn't seem to be any way to open it! It doesn't have a lid that you can lift or sides that open. It doesn't even seem to have a top and a bottom. How to open it was a mystery to me! I certainly was puzzled!

I'm going to let you look at it more closely now. Maybe you will find a clue to the mystery. *(Give the box to a child to examine and to pass on to another.)* Please handle it carefully and gently. Don't push or pull hard on any part of it because it might break if you do.

I said that how to open the box was a mystery to me. What does that word "mystery" mean? *(Something we don't understand.)* Does anyone here like to read mysteries or listen to someone reading a mystery? The kind of mysteries we find in books are usually stories about something strange or mysterious that has happened. A detective might have to look for clues to help to solve the mystery. There are board games, too, where you can play at figuring out mysteries. Have you ever played a game like that?

Have you ever heard the words "holy mystery"? What do you think a holy mystery would be? Do you know what "holy" means? It doesn't mean that something has holes in it. This word "holy" means "coming from God." So a holy mystery is something coming from God that we don't understand.

Let's hear what the apostle Paul wrote about a mystery. He was in prison when he wrote to the people—the church—in a city called Colosse. Listen for the word "mystery." *(Read aloud Colossians 1:25–27.)* Paul wrote that God gave him special work to do. That work was for him to become a servant of the church and to tell the people what God teaches. This teaching was a mystery, a secret that was hidden from everyone since the beginning of time. But then God decided to let God's people know the mystery—the secret truth. The mystery is Jesus Christ, who comes to live in your heart when you invite him in!

Paul wanted the believers to pray that he might have a chance to tell many people the mystery of Christ in them, even though that's why he was put into prison in the first place.

So, according to Paul, God's mystery—a holy mystery—is Jesus Christ living in us. Is that a mystery to you? What do you know about Jesus? God's plan—a holy mystery—was to have his child Jesus live on earth in a human body. Jesus would be right in everything he did. He never did anything wrong that to God was a sin. Yet, he died for the wrongs that we do. He rose again and was taken into heaven. God's plan is to have Jesus Christ live in the hearts of everyone who believes in him.

Do you think you know everything there is to know about Jesus and the holy mystery? Do you think there is anyone here who knows everything there is to know about Jesus and the holy mystery? Our minds can never understand the mind and the mystery of God.

The good news for all of us is that we don't need to understand the holy mystery. All we have to do is believe and trust that God loves us; God's child, Jesus, died for us so that we can live forever with him; and when we invite him in, Jesus lives in our hearts

May I please have my puzzle box now? Has anyone figured out how to open it without breaking it? (*Demonstrate opening.*) This week you may find or read or hear about a mystery—something that puzzles you, something you don't understand. What will you do when that happens? (*Look for clues to help you solve the mystery; ask a friend or a grown-up for help; pray that God will help you to understand what you need to know.*) Let that mystery remind you of the holy mystery of Jesus living in you.

OPTIONAL: STRETCHING FURTHER

Read the closing of Paul's letter to the Romans (16:25–7). Note that this is a "doxology"—a praise to God—ending with an exclamation mark to show strong feeling. Paul exclaims that it's wonderful to be alive when the mystery—God's secret—is becoming known throughout the world!

Let's pray. (*Ask children to bow their heads and repeat after you. Say short, meaningful phrases.*)

Dear God, thank you for sending Jesus to us. We do not understand your holy mystery, but we believe in him. So we know he lives in our hearts. He is helping us to live and give as he does. Thank you, God. Thank you, Jesus. Amen.

15
A New Beginning

THEME: Use God's special gift to you to do something good for everyone.

SCRIPTURE: Now there are varieties of gifts, but the same Spirit; and there are varieties of services, but the same Lord; and there are varieties of activities, but it is the same God who activates all of them in everyone. To each is given the manifestation of the Spirit for the common good.—1 Corinthians 12:4–7

PREPARATION: Obtain a flashlight in good, working condition. Take it apart and put the pieces in a bag, box, or backpack.

---

*I'm getting ready to go on a camping retreat. One of the things I need to take along is a flashlight, so I asked my son if I could borrow his. "Sure," he said, "I'll get it for you." A few minutes later, he handed me this. (*Indicate bag.*) I should warn you that he likes to play jokes on me. Who wants to turn on the flashlight? (*Hand the bag to a volunteer.*)

What's wrong? Can't you turn it on? What a joke on me! There are only pieces of a flashlight in the bag! Who knows how to put it together? (*Let one or several children together try to assemble the flashlight while you continue talking.*)

Today we're going to talk about new beginnings. (*Ask what new groups the children might attend soon for the first time, such as a day-care class; a school; a first-, second-, or third-grade class; a scout troop; a sports team; a Sunday-school class.*) Is this a new church for anyone?

How do you feel about being in a new group or in a new place? Are you happy and excited? Are you a little worried or afraid? *I know a boy who was scared to go to kindergarten because he didn't know how to read. He didn't know that most children don't learn to read until after they have finished kindergarten.

Do you think, in your new group, whatever it may be, that everyone will be able to do everything well? Will everyone be able to stay inside the lines when you color something? Will everyone use scissors well? Might someone be good at drawing, and someone else be a good runner? Could someone be a good listener, and someone else be a good storyteller? Maybe one person is good at working with numbers, and another person is good at making things with his or her hands. Could someone be a good pitcher, and someone else be a good hitter?

Wouldn't your group be dull and boring if everyone were alike and did everything exactly the same way? I'm glad God has a better plan. Do you know what God's plan is? Listen to what the apostle Paul wrote about God's plan. *(Read aloud 1 Corinthians 12:4–7.)* God gives different kinds of gifts. God gives each of us a special gift, not a package wrapped in pretty paper, but something we can do well. God wants us to use that gift to do something good for everyone.

Have you ever helped to put on a program or a play for an audience? *When I taught fifth grade, I liked to have my class put on a play. Each person in the class needed to do something well in order for the play to be a success. Some students memorized parts and acted as characters in the play. Others were prompters. They followed the script and, if an actor forgot what to say, the prompter whispered it. Some students drew murals or scenery for the backdrop. Someone opened and closed the curtain. Someone signed our name on the schedule for using the stage to practice. Others made invitations to give to other classes and parents to come to see the play.

Everyone had a job to do. The job of the person who pulled the curtain was as important as the job of the actor who memorized the most lines. The job of the person who scheduled the stage was as important as the one who drew scenery. When everyone did their jobs well, the class put on a good play. If only one person was absent, the whole play was affected. At the end, the actors took bows while the audience clapped; but everyone deserved applause, not only the actors.

In your new group, there may be someone who does well at something that you don't do very well. Suppose a teammate almost always gets a hit when he or she comes up to bat, and you almost always strike out. Should you feel jealous? No. Maybe you could ask that person to show you how to do better.

Perhaps someone in your class always knows the answers to the teacher's questions. Maybe *you* are that person. Should you feel proud of what you can do? You can feel good if you have studied and worked hard to learn what you know. Be sure to thank God that you are able to learn and remember well. You should not be jealous or proud of the gifts God gives.

God's plan is good. God gave each of us a special gift, something that each of us can do well, something important. God looks at all of us as equals. One person or one person's work is not more important than another's work.

God planned to give each believer in Jesus a special gift so that everyone would work well together in the church, doing the work of Jesus. When people use their gifts well in a group and every member does his or her part, the family, the class, the team, or the church works as God planned.

Who has the flashlight? (*If the children have been able to put it together, commend them for using their gifts well. If they have been unsuccessful, show how each part fits together so the flashlight works as intended.*)

The next time you are asked to do a job, remember the flashlight. Every part of it needs to be in the right place, and every part needs to do its job well, or the flashlight won't give any light. Remember that your work, your part in your team, class, church, and family is important. Do it well and do it gladly.

OPTIONAL: STRETCHING FURTHER
Maybe you haven't discovered God's gift to you yet. As you grow up, your parents, your pastor, your teachers, and your friends can help you to find out what your special gift is. Don't forget to ask God! God, the One who gave you the gift, is the One who knows best of all!

Let's pray. (*Ask children to bow their heads and repeat after you. Say short, meaningful phrases.*)

Dear God, we thank you for giving us different gifts. Help us to use them to work together. We want to do something good for everyone. In Jesus' name. Amen.

16
Singing Hearts

THEME: Praise God with a song in your heart.

SCRIPTURE: Sing psalms and hymns and spiritual songs among yourselves, singing and making melody to the Lord in your hearts, giving thanks to God the Father at all times and for everything in the name of our Lord Jesus Christ.

—Ephesians 5:19–20

PREPARATION: 1. Locate words and music for several familiar children's songs, appropriate for the above theme. Suggestions are: "Praise Him, Praise Him!"; "Happy All the Way"; "Sing and Smile and Pray"; and "In My Heart There Rings a Melody." 2. If you wish, prearrange for a choir member or director to sit with you and the children and lead them in singing. 3. Mark the first and last pages of the Psalms in your Bible.

How are you today? Is everyone happy? Is anyone happy? Would you like to tell us why you're happy?

*I'm sorry to say that I wasn't feeling especially happy before I came here today. I think maybe I got up on the wrong side of the bed. Nothing seemed to go right. I found a hole in the stockings I wanted to wear. I spilled my juice. I couldn't find my car keys. I left my offering envelope on the kitchen table. Has that ever happened to you—everything seemed to go wrong from the time you got up in the morning?

My friend told me what happened at her house when she was grumpy in the morning. Her mother would tell her to go back to bed, stay there for ten minutes, and then get up on the other side of the bed and start the day all over again.

When you're feeling grumpy, or sad, or lonely, what can you do so that you'll feel better? I learned something in the Bible that helps me. I learned it from David in the psalms that he wrote. Do you know what psalms are? They are sacred songs or poems that people use in worshiping God. There are a lot of psalms in the Bible. (*Open to the first and last psalms and show the many pages on which psalms have been printed.*) Do you know how many psalms there are in the book of Psalms? There are 150 psalms. Listen to what David said in Psalm 27. (*Read aloud Psalm 27:6b.*) David said, "I will sing and make melody to the Lord."

The first thing I want to do when I am feeling bad or sad is to talk to God. I can do that by singing to God. I might sing a happy song, even if I don't feel happy before I start to sing. Guess what happens! I begin to feel happy because I have started to sing! The more I sing, the happier I feel. I think that, the happier I feel, the happier the people around me are, too. They like being near me much better when I am happy than when I am grumpy.

Let's try singing together! (*Lead the children in singing "Praise Him, Praise Him!" or a song of praise familiar to the children.*)

Is it working? How do you feel? We worship and talk to God through our song, and we praise God with our melody. Through music we lift one another up.

I found something else in the Bible about singing. It's in a letter that the apostle Paul wrote to the believers in Jesus at Ephesus. (*Read aloud Ephesians 5:19–20.*) Did you notice that Paul wrote about "singing and making melody to the Lord in your hearts"? I wondered what he meant. A melody is a sweet song that we are pleased to hear. How can we make a melody, a song, in our hearts? In the Bible, we often find that the word "heart" means what's inside you, the most important part of you. Have you ever heard a song singing or playing inside you, in your mind, but no one else could hear it? The melody sings itself over and over in your heart.

So we can sing to God in two ways. We can sing out loud, and we can make melody in our hearts. Even when it's not a good time for us to sing out loud, we can still sing in our hearts. When we sing to God, we make God happy, we help to make one another happy, and we make ourselves glad.

There is a part of Paul's letter that we haven't talked about. Listen closely to the last part of the message. (*Read again Ephesians 5: 19–20.*) Besides singing, what did the apostle Paul tell the people to do? (*Give thanks.*) When should they give thanks? (*At all times.*) For what should they thank God? (*For everything.*) What can you think of that *you* want to thank God for?

I already feel much better than I did when I got up on the wrong side of the bed this morning. How about you? This week, I hope you will keep a song in your heart. Praise God and thank God with your singing. Look for people who need *you* to be kind to them.

OPTIONAL: STRETCHING FURTHER

Here's another way to make yourself and others glad. Have you ever been so unhappy that you felt sorry for yourself? Maybe you couldn't have something you really wanted. Maybe you weren't allowed to go somewhere or to play with someone who wanted to play with you. I found that a way to stop feeling sorry for myself is to look for someone who needs help. Then do something good for that person. I might bake some cookies or a pie for my neighbor who can't make them for himself. I might offer a ride to someone who will be going to the same place that I'm going. Soon, I have stopped feeling sorry for *me*, and I'm glad to help someone else. Can *you* think of anyone who needs *your* help? Who needs *you* to be kind? Who needs *your* love? Who needs *your* hands and feet to do something? Best of all, when we do something for others, it's like doing something for Jesus.

Let's pray. Please bow your heads, close your eyes, and repeat after me. (*Say short, meaningful phrases.*)

Dear God, we thank you for songs to sing. We praise you for the melody in our hearts. Help us to do something good for someone every day in Jesus' name. Amen.

Let's leave with a song on our lips and a melody in our hearts today. (*Lead the children and the congregation, if you wish, in singing "In My Heart There Rings a Melody" or another song familiar to the children.*)

17
Apple Seeds

THEME: Children can help to plant seeds of faith.

SCRIPTURE: The seed is the word of God.—Luke 8:11b

PREPARATION: Bring a knife and enough apples to give one to each child. You may want to wash or wipe them in case the children want to eat them before going home.

I brought apples today. Aren't they beautiful? Do you like apples? I like to see the trees hanging heavy with fruit ready for picking. I think I can almost taste them, fresh and crisp and juicy, while they are still on the trees.

*When I was a little girl, apple trees were special to me. I liked to climb the trees close to our house. My dad hung a swing seat from ropes over a strong branch. I liked to swing back and forth as high as I could go.

In the springtime, white blossoms covered the trees. Soon, little green apples began to grow. When they grew big and ripe, I helped my mother to make applesauce. We filled glass jars with it to eat in wintertime.

Then I grew up and got married and had children of my own. By this time, Mother liked to put her home-cooked applesauce in the freezer instead of canning it. Often, when we visited her, she had forgotten to get the sauce out of the freezer soon enough for it to thaw by dinnertime. That was fine with my children. They sometimes argued over who would get the icy part in the middle of the bowl!

Have you ever heard "an apple a day keeps the doctor away"? It's an old saying. We know that apples don't have any magic power to keep you from getting sick. They do have vitamins and minerals that your body needs to be healthy.

Apples still fascinate me. Do you know what is in the middle of an apple? The middle part of the apple is called the core. There are seeds in the center. Let's see. (*Cut an apple into quarters and expose the seeds. Let the children count them.*) Do you think all apples have the same number of seeds? (*No.*)

Why is it important for apples to have seeds? God's plan seems almost like a miracle, doesn't it? From a small seed, a tree grows, and not just any kind of tree, but the same kind of tree on which this apple grew. It will have the same kind of leaves, the same kind of flowers, and the same kind of bark. The tree that grows from this seed then produces the same kind of apples with seeds, and the cycle goes on. Someone said that we can count the seeds in an apple, but only God can count the apples in a seed. Only God knows how many more trees and how many more apples will grow from one seed. There are so many that we can't count them!

We can read in the Bible a story that Jesus told about seeds. Jesus told about a man who scattered, or sowed, seed on the ground. The man was called a sower. Listen to what happened to the seed in Jesus' story. (*Read aloud Luke 8:5–8.*) What happened to the seed? Did all of it grow? Some seed was stepped on, and the birds ate some of it. Other seed fell on the rock, and it couldn't grow there. Some seed fell among thorns, and the thorns choked the plants. Did any of it grow well? Yes, some seed fell on good soil and produced one hundred times as much seed as was scattered.

Jesus' disciples asked him what the story meant.

Jesus said, "The seed is the word of God." He told them that some people hear God's word, but they don't believe it. Some people believe it, but for only a little while. When trouble comes, they stop believing. Other people hear God's word, but they get so busy with other things that God's word can't grow in them. They never get around to doing anything about God's teaching. Some people with willing hearts hear God's word and hold on to it. They obey God's laws, and they follow Jesus. They are like apple trees, putting down roots and spreading their branches. They produce good fruit by loving their neighbors and sharing the good news of God's word. The seed—God's word—then grows in those people, and they, in turn, plant God's word in still others.

You are growing like seeds in good soil when you come to worship to listen to God's word and to learn in your Sunday school classes and middle-of-the-week get-togethers. When you obey God's word, your faith grows. You learn more and more about loving God and how God wants you to love others.

Do you know that you can help to plant seeds for God? Do you know someone in your neighborhood or in your school or day care who doesn't go to church? Talk it over with your parents. If it's all right with them, you could invite that person to come to church with you. Tell her or him how much fun you have here and what you are learning about Jesus.

Telling someone about Jesus or asking someone to come with you to worship is one way you can help to plant seeds for God. If even one person comes with you and accepts Jesus' love and learns to follow him, that person will be like good seed growing in good soil. That person can invite someone else, and it will become a good harvest for God. It's important for apples to have seeds that will grow more apples. It's important, too, for the church to plant seeds to grow, with so many people living like Jesus that we can't count them.

OPTIONAL: STRETCHING FURTHER
Read aloud 2 Corinthians 9:6. Explain that one who plants only a few seeds will get a small harvest or crop. One who plants many seeds will get a big harvest. We need to keep on inviting and bringing people to church. Wouldn't it be great if everyone, including grownups, here today, brought one new person to church next week?

Let's pray. Please bow your heads and repeat after me. (Say short, meaningful phrases.)

Dear God, thank you for apples. Thank you for seeds to grow more apples. Help us to plant seeds for you. Help us to tell someone how much you love us. In Jesus' name. Amen.

(Give each child an apple.) I hope this apple will help you to remember Jesus' story about seeds. You can count the seeds in your apple. Remember to tell someone about Jesus and invite someone to come to church with you next week.

18
For the Birds

THEME: God cares for God's creatures, including you!

SCRIPTURE: So do not be afraid; you are of more value than many sparrows.—Matthew 10:31

PREPARATION: Obtain a guide to field identification of birds or photos of sparrows and finches. Use doughnut-shaped cereal and 10- to 12-inch pieces of string to make one garland per child.

Did you ever wake up to hear birds singing? I like to hear the birds singing as they wake up, and as I wake up to a new day.

Do you think God cares about birds? Can we learn anything from the Bible about whether God cares about birds? First of all, who made the birds when the world was being made? Listen to Genesis, the first book of the Bible. (*Read aloud Genesis 1:20–22.*) What did God make? God made every living creature that moves. God created great sea monsters and every winged bird of every kind. What did God think of the creatures that God had made? God saw that it was good, and God blessed them. God made fish to fill the waters and birds to fill the sky.

Now let's look at the book of Psalms. In Psalm 104, the writer tells how great God is. The writer praises God for the many things God has created in the world where we live. Listen to find out what places God provided for birds to build their homes. (*Read aloud Psalm 104:12 and 104:16–17.*) Where do birds build their nests? (*In trees, by streams.*)

Did God make all the living things and then forget about them? God provides the food they need to live on, too. (*Read aloud Psalm*

104:27.) All creatures depend on God for food. What do birds eat? (*Seeds, insects, earthworms, fish, berries, or fruit, depending on the kind of bird.*)

What did Jesus say about birds? (*Read aloud Matthew 6:26.*) Jesus reminded the people that God feeds the birds. Then he added that people are worth much more to God than birds!

At another time, Jesus talked about sparrows. Do you know what sparrows look like? (*Show pictures in a reference book.*) Sparrows are small, mostly brown, twittering birds. They are plentiful in many parts of the world. Listen to what Jesus said about sparrows to the apostles. (*Read aloud Matthew 10:29 and 10:31.*) If you wanted to buy a sparrow, how much would it cost? Jesus said that you could buy two sparrows for only a penny. Sparrows aren't worth much money, but God cares so much for these common, little birds that he knows when even one of them dies.

Since God cares so much for birds, we should also treat them with respect and care. *One day my neighbor asked me to come to help a bird that was trapped in a lilac bush. It was a gray finch. (*Show picture.*) Its feet were tangled in a piece of fishing line that was wrapped around a branch. The bird flapped its wings, but it couldn't fly away. My neighbor, wearing gloves, gently held the bird while I cut the nylon line. She opened her hands and the bird chirped loudly and flew away. Then we noticed that several other finches had been waiting and watching from an evergreen tree nearby. A cat had also been hiding under the tree. It ran off after the bird flew away. Sometimes, we can be the hands and feet of God, helping to care for and to save what God has created.

Listen again to verse 31. (*Reread Matthew 10:31.*) There is a song that says, "For his eye is on the sparrow, and I know he watches me." *You* are worth much more to God than a whole flock of sparrows. Jesus said that you don't need to worry or be afraid. (*Read aloud Matthew 6:25a.*) God will provide what you need.

God provides for you in another way, too. (*Read aloud John 3:16.*) God cares so much for you that God sent his only son to take the punishment for the wrong things you have done. Jesus, who never did anything wrong, died to save you. As my neighbor and I set the bird free, we can trust Jesus to set us free, too, so that we can live forever with him.

Does anyone have a bird feeder near where you live? Putting out seeds for birds to eat can be a way to help them, especially when it's too cold for plants to grow or the ground is covered with snow. Here's another way to feed birds. (*Give each child a cereal garland.*) You can hang this cereal garland on a bush. Maybe you would like to make garlands at home. You will need cereal with a hole in the middle. Take a long piece of string and poke it through the holes, as though you are making a necklace. Maybe your family and friends would like to make them, too. Wouldn't it be fun to look outside when you're having your breakfast cereal and see the birds eating their cereal, too? Then think about the many ways God takes care of you, too.

OPTIONAL: STRETCHING FURTHER

What kinds of things can trap us and keep us from being the best we can be? (*Always wanting to have your way, being untruthful, being upset at losing a game, envying someone who has more than you do, not wanting to share.*)

Let's pray. (*Remind children to bow their heads and repeat after you. Say short, meaningful phrases.*)

Dear God, thank you for making birds. Thank you for watching over them. We know that you watch over us, too. Thank you for caring for us. Help us to trust you. In Jesus' name. Amen.

19
A Feast for the Eyes

THEME: God made us all in God's image, and we are all beautiful in God's sight.

SCRIPTURE: So God created humankind in his image, in the image of God he created them; male and female he created them.—Genesis 1:27

PREPARATION: 1. Gather leaves of different colors: green, yellow, brown, red, orange, and purple. If your locale does not have leaves with changing colors, use another "natural wonder" (birds of various colors; zoo animals; desert flowers blooming in spring; or rainbows) as an example of God's beautiful creation. 2. Obtain a set of crayons with unusual colors or color samples from a paint store.

Have you noticed what is happening to the leaves outside? (*They are falling and changing colors.*) What do you like to do with leaves? (*Kick them while walking to hear their rustling sound; rake them; put them in piles; jump into a pile of them; toss them upward on a windy day.*)

I brought some leaves that I picked up. What color were the leaves in summer? What colors do you see now? Do you know why we see different colors in fall?

During the summer, the leaves were green because of something inside them called chlorophyll. Sunlight and water help the chlorophyll make sugar and starch that the tree needs to grow. In fall, we don't have as much daylight as in summer, and nights are cooler. Where the leaf stem fastens onto the tree branch, a tough layer like cork grows. (*Show end of leaf stem.*) Then the sugar and starch—the tree's food—can't get to the leaf. Because there isn't as much chlorophyll, the green color fades. Soon, the other colors that were under the green layer begin to show.

Do you know who made the trees and their leaves? Listen to what the Bible tells us. *(Read aloud Genesis 1:11.)* What do you think that word "vegetation" means? "Vegetation" means plants. On the third day, when God made the world we live in, God made plants—little plants and big plants, like trees. God made each plant to have seeds that will become more of its own kind of plant.

God made leaves. Will you say that with me? "God made leaves." I'm going to hold up one kind of leaf at a time. We're going to add one more word to what we say. Here's a green leaf. Let's say, "God made green leaves." *(Continue holding up one leaf at a time, while children chant as above, inserting the appropriate color word, such as yellow, orange, red, purple, brown. Conclude the exercise by holding up all the leaves and saying, "God made all kinds of leaves.")*

Do you know what a "feast" is? A feast is a big dinner with lots of good food. When might you have a feast? We might have a feast on Thanksgiving Day or when we're celebrating something special. That's a feast for the stomach. What do you think a feast for the eyes might be? A feast for the eyes is something that is very beautiful and wonderful to see. I think that the changing colors of fall leaves are a feast for the eyes. I think colorful leaves are a feast for God's eyes, too. Let's say together "Colorful leaves are a feast for God's eyes." Now let's say "Colorful leaves are a feast for our eyes."

What else can you think of that God made with different colors to be a feast for the eyes? *(Rainbows, birds, flowers, rocks.)* How many different colors do you think God made in the whole universe? I brought a set of samples from a store that sells wall paint. *(Show.)* How many different colors would you guess are in this whole pack of cards? There are more than 700 in this set! Let's look at the blue cards. There are more than 120 shades of blue here. Do you think that someone has made even more shades of these colors? I think God, who created color, has made and continues to make more kinds of color than we can imagine.

Now let's think about people. Do we all look alike? Do we all have the same color eyes? Hair? Skin? I tried to find a paint chip that looks exactly like my skin. I couldn't find one.

Did God make us, too? Let's look at Genesis again. *(Read aloud Genesis 1:27.)* On the sixth day, God made "humankind." That means human beings—people: men and women, boys and girls. Let's hear what God thought about God's creation. *(Read aloud Genesis 1:31.)*

Do you think God likes one kind of person—one color of person—better than another?

God made each one of us different. All together, we are a feast for God's eyes. Not only do we look different, but God gave each of us a special gift—something we will be able to do well. God loves each one of us as though there was only one of us—as though we were the only person in the world. God loves you as though God had no one else in the whole world for a friend. If God loves everyone, then we ought to love one another.

God also made us all alike in many ways. Can you think of a way that you are like every other person? What happens if you get a cut on your knee? What happens if you stay in the sun too long? What do you do when you get sleepy? Do you want to stay all your life the same size you are today? (*All children bleed red blood, get sunburned, yawn, want to grow up, get hungry and thirsty, get hiccups, and catch a cold.*) But it is the way God made us to be different that makes each one of us special.

I'm going to give each of you a (*crayon or*) paint card with lots of colors on it. I hope it will help you to remember that God created colors. God made the world and everything in it—plants, animals, and people. God made us all. God loves every one of us, and, even though we are all different, we ought to love one another.

OPTIONAL: STRETCHING FURTHER
Read again Genesis 1:27. How can we be "God's image"? (*We can reflect God's nature by being loving, kind, patient, forgiving, and faithful.*)

Let's pray. (*Remind children to bow their heads and repeat after you. Say short, meaningful phrases.*)

Dear God, thank you for beautiful colors. Thank you for making us all different. Help us to love one another. We pray in Jesus' name. Amen.

20
No Change

THEME: God does not change. We can always rely on God, who loves us.

SCRIPTURE: For I the Lord do not change.—Malachi 3:6a

PREPARATION: 1. Gather about four photos of yourself or a family member in various stages of life. 2. If possible, obtain a memento—an item reminiscent of that person's life and love. 3. Obtain stickers, bookmarks, or small crosses to give to each child as a reminder of God's love.

Before we begin today, I am going to make a promise to you. I promise to give you something after we pray. Will you remind me? Thank you.

I brought some pictures to show you today. Move close to me so you can see. What do you see in this first photo? (*A baby.*) Do you think this baby is a girl or a boy? How can you tell? (*Continue showing the photos chronologically. Encourage children to estimate the subject's age in each one. They may or may not be aware that all of the photos are of the same person. If they do not guess this is so after seeing the last photo, tell them.*) Did you know that the same person was in all of the pictures? How did you know (*or why did you not guess*) that it was the same person?

We change a lot from the time we are babies until we are "senior citizens." What changes did you notice in these photos?

*I have something else to show you. This is a box for keeping thread and needles for sewing. I remember that I gave it to my mother at Christmas when I was a teenager. She liked to sew. She made dresses for my sister and me. She liked to make rugs and quilts, too. (*Show something that she made: a braided or hooked rug, a quilt, an embroidered pillowcase, a crocheted item.*) Mother showed that she loved us by the things she made and gave to us.

I have this sewing box now because my mother has died and gone to be with Jesus. I keep my sewing supplies in it now. This box reminds me that I loved my mother and my mother loved me. You noticed in the photos how she changed as she grew older. But one thing did not change--she always loved her family, and she always loved God.

We learn in the Bible about God's love. (*Read aloud 1 John 4:7–8.*) God's Word says that God is love. Do you think if I found the word "God" in the dictionary, it would say that "God" means love? No. Love is what God does. Love comes from God.

We learn something else about God from God's prophet and messenger, Malachi. (*Read aloud Malachi 3:6a.*) God never changes. God is invisible to us. We can't see God, but if we could take a picture of God, God would be the same from the beginning of creation throughout "forever."

I promised to give you something this morning. If I don't keep my promise, how will you feel? If I do keep the promise, how will you feel? We can believe that God will do what God promises. God's Word is like God. It doesn't change. We can always count on God because God loves us.

At the time when Malachi spoke God's Word, the people had broken God's laws and done bad things. God was not happy with the people, but God didn't stop loving them. God said, "Return to me and I will return to you" (Malachi 3:7). To know God is to obey God's commandments. If we know God, we will love others as God does. Who is our example for living and loving? We must love and serve one another as Jesus did. Jesus showed us what God is like.

The sewing box reminds me that I loved my mother and she loved me. What do we have to remind us that God loves us? Look around. What do you see? (*The cross, the Bible, hymnals, a choir, musical instruments, murals, stained glass windows, parents, teachers, preachers, bread and wine.*) Let these things all help you to remember: God loves you. (*Hand out small remembrances of God's love.*)

OPTIONAL: STRETCHING FURTHER

Have you heard or read any Bible stories that tell how Jesus showed his love? What did Jesus do? (*Jesus healed sick people: made a paralyzed man walk; made a blind man see; and made a mute man speak. He brought dead people back to life. Jesus fed thousands of hungry people. He washed his disciples' feet. He gave his life to pay for our sins. He died on the cross and forgave those who killed him.*) No one can ever love us more than Jesus does.

Let's pray. (*Ask children to bow their heads and repeat after you. Say short, meaningful phrases.*)

Dear God, we want to know you and love you. Forgive us for the wrong things we have done. Help us to obey your laws. We will often think of you. Help us to give you our best every day. We pray in Jesus' name. Amen.

21
God Calls

THEME: God calls to us in the small choices of each day.

SCRIPTURE: Now the Lord came and stood there, calling as before, "Samuel! Samuel!" And Samuel said, "Speak, for your servant is listening."—1 Samuel 3:10

PREPARATION: Obtain a hunter's call for turkey, duck, deer, elk, moose, or fox.

I brought something today that lets me make a strange sound. (*Demonstrate.*) Have you ever heard that sound before? It is supposed to sound like a wild turkey. Who might use this turkey call? A hunter uses it to call a turkey close enough for the hunter to see him.

You know that different animals make different sounds. Animals listen for the sounds that they know. Do you have a pet? Does your pet know the sound of your voice? Does your pet know the sound of the name you have given him or her? When you call your pet, does your pet come to you?

The Bible tells us about a young boy who heard his name being called. But, first, let me tell you about his mother, Hannah. Before she had children, Hannah was so unhappy that she couldn't eat. At the tabernacle—the special tent where the people worshiped God—she cried and prayed that God would give her a son. She promised that, if she had a son, she would give the boy back to God for as long as he lived. Can you imagine wanting something very much, getting it, and then giving it back to the one who gave it to you?

God answered Hannah's prayer and, in time, a baby boy was born to her and her husband. They named him Samuel.

Hannah kept her promise. When Samuel was about three years old, his mother took him to the tabernacle. Hannah left him there with the priest, Eli, who would teach Samuel how to serve God.

Each year, Samuel grew bigger, and each year, he outgrew his clothes. He missed his family, but he knew that his mother would make new clothes and bring them when she came to see him.

One night, Samuel was in bed in the tabernacle when he heard someone calling his name. Samuel thought it was Eli calling him. He said, "Here I am!" Let's hear the Bible story in the book called First Samuel. *(Read aloud 1 Samuel 3:5–6.)* Now Samuel had been learning about God, but he had never heard God's voice speaking to him. *(Read aloud 1 Samuel 3:8–10.)*

What did Samuel say when God called his name again? Let's all say it together: "Speak, for your servant is listening."

God gave a message to Samuel. It was about Eli's sons. They were priests, too, but they had not obeyed God's laws, and they had not obeyed their father. The message to Samuel was that God would punish Eli's sons. Samuel did not want to tell Eli, but Eli asked what God had said. Later on, it happened, and Eli's sons were punished.

Samuel, however, was like a good and wise son to Eli and a faithful servant of God. God trusted Samuel to listen whenever God spoke to him. What did God trust Samuel to do? *(Listen.)* Samuel became a prophet whom the people of Israel trusted. The messages that God spoke through him always came true. Samuel became a great man of God.

Have you ever heard God calling your name? From the story of Samuel, we learn that God does call children. We might expect that God would have given the message to Eli, the priest who had served and known God for many years. But God works at any place, at any time, and through anyone, God chooses, even children. God knew Samuel's name; God knows your name, too.

When Samuel first heard his name being called, he didn't know it was God's voice. We might not recognize God's voice, either. So we must learn to hear God. We can do that by hearing and reading God's word in the Bible. When we pray, we thank God for the good things God gives us. We tell God what we care about. We ask God to help us. Then we must be quiet and listen. What did God trust Samuel to do? *(Listen.)* Wouldn't it be terrible if God was speaking, but no one was listening?

God doesn't always speak in a voice that we can hear with our ears. More often, we "hear" God's voice in our hearts. God's voice is that something inside us that tells us the right thing to do. God calls to us, children and grown-ups, in the small choices of each day.

God calls you to obey your parents and your teachers. God calls you to be honest and kind. God calls you to be a good friend, a good neighbor, a good worker, and a good helper.

When you need to make a choice, you should recognize God's call and answer as Samuel did. What was Samuel's answer? Let's say it together again: "Speak, for your servant is listening."

This week, I hope you will take some time every day to be quiet and listen. Turn off the television, the radio, and the CD player. Talk to God and listen for God's voice. God is always listening for your voice.

OPTIONAL: STRETCHING FURTHER

Imagine this is happening to you. Listen for God's voice in your heart:

1. A woman walks across a parking lot near a supermarket. You see that she has dropped something. You pick it up. It's a five-dollar bill. What should you do?

2. Your cousins come to visit. You want to play your new game with them. They want to play the same old game you always play with them. What should you do?

3. Your children's choir meets at church on Tuesday to practice the songs you will sing on Sunday. The children have all arrived, but the choir leader is late. The room is big enough for running races. The chairs make great jumping-off spots. There are lots of good hiding places, too. What should you do?

Let's pray. (*Ask children to bow their heads and repeat after you. Say short, meaningful phrase.*)

Dear God, thank you for calling Samuel when he was a boy. Help me to learn, as he did, to listen when you speak. Help me to obey and be the kind of person you want me to be. Thank you for listening to me. In Jesus' name. Amen.

22
Finding the Way

THEME: Jesus shows us the way to God the Father.

SCRIPTURE: "I am the way, and the truth, and the life. No one comes to the Father except through me."—John 14:6

PREPARATION: Bring a compass and a road map or a printout from a computer program, such as MapQuest, showing driving directions from your home to the church. Cut an old map into 3-inch squares (or obtain small, computer-printed maps) to give to each child.

---

*I had a dream last night. It was not a good, happy dream. I dreamed that I was supposed to go somewhere, and I could see, far ahead of me, the place where I was supposed to go. But I didn't know how to get there. I didn't know the way. I kept going around and around in circles, always ending up at the same place where I started.

Has that ever happened to you? Have you ever been lost? What happened?

Have you ever been traveling with your family when the driver got lost and didn't know which way to go? Who gets lost more often, Mom or Dad? What happens when your family gets lost? What do they do? How do grown-ups find out how to get to where they're going? (*Show maps.*) A map can help us find the way. How else can we get directions? (*Ask someone for directions; follow someone who knows the way.*) Which way is the best way to get to where you are going? (*The latter.*)

Another method of getting to where you want to go is called orienteering. You use a map and a compass (*Show.*) at your starting place. You make a mark, perhaps on a tree ahead, in the direction you should go. When you reach that tree, you use the compass again, mark another distant tree, and keep on doing that. If you have walked in the right direction, you will reach your destination.

*I remember a time, however, when I took my fifth-grade class orienteering. A college student led us and showed us what to do. We walked and walked, uphill and through a thick forest. Lunchtime came, but we had not arrived at the spot where we would meet the other classes.

Can you guess what we did? We did exactly what we had been told to do if we got lost. We had come to a road. We just stood there and yelled, "Help!" The other children and teachers heard us and found us. We really weren't very far from them, but we were embarrassed. We discovered that we had not begun our hike at exactly the right spot. Even though we had followed our leader's directions, we couldn't end up at the right place because we hadn't started at the right spot.

In the Bible, Jesus tells us about finding the way. He had told his disciples that he would soon leave them and go to his home in heaven. His disciples were sad about the things that Jesus had said would happen to him. Listen to what Jesus told them. (Read aloud John 14:1–4.) Jesus was trying to comfort them, but Thomas didn't understand. (Read aloud John 14:5–6.)

We said the best way to find how to get somewhere is to follow someone who knows the way. Christians—those who believe in Jesus Christ—always have Jesus to show the way. Jesus said, "I am the way." He said, "Follow me" (John 21:22b). He said, "Trust me" (John 14:1). Jesus said that he is the only way to God.

How can we follow Jesus if we can't see him? Jesus left us a map. Do you know what we call that map? It's the Bible. The Bible—God's Word—tells us how Jesus lived, how much he loves us, and why he died for us. Jesus gave us directions. (Read aloud John 15:12 and John 15:14.) When we trust Jesus and obey his directions to love one another and to obey his commandments, we are walking on the path that takes us to God. God sends other people, too, like parents, grandparents, teachers, pastors, and friends to help us find the way.

Another way to be sure that we are following Jesus is to talk with the One who created this world, where we sometimes feel lost. How can we do that? (Pray.) Do you know that Jesus is the only person in the Bible who invites us to pray to him, in his name? He is always ready to help you, whenever you pray, wherever you pray, and however you pray. So, if you feel lost, you don't need to be afraid. You can talk with the One who made the map and the One who is the way!

We talked about what to do to get to where you're going. First, decide where you want to go. We Christians are on a journey to Almighty God. Follow someone who knows the way. For us, that person is Jesus. Get directions. Jesus left us a map, the Bible. The Bible points the way, like a compass, and gives us directions. We can get directions, too, from other followers of Jesus, the church. We have still another way to get directions, by praying—talking and listening to God—and remembering that Jesus said, "I am the way."

I am going to give you a small map (*or a piece of a map*) to put in your pocket. I hope it will remind you that Jesus is the way to God. Remember to obey his commandments and to love one another.

OPTIONAL: STRETCHING FURTHER
Sometimes we feel "lost," even when we are not actually lost. Have you ever felt that way? (*Examples: not knowing how to do something, such as tying your shoelaces or making a computer do what you want it to do; not knowing what to do or say in a situation.*) Did you find help? How could you find help?

Let's pray. (*Ask children to bow their heads and repeat after you. Say short, meaningful phrases.*)

Dear Jesus, we are happy to know that you are the way to God. With you as our guide, we don't need to be afraid. Help us to follow you every day. We pray in your name. Amen.

23
Whiter Than Snow

THEME: When we are sorry for the wrongs we have done, and we ask God to forgive us, God wipes away our sin.

SCRIPTURE: Wash me, and I shall be whiter than snow.
—Psalm 51:7b

PREPARATION: If you are in a region where there is no snow, perhaps you can obtain a photograph of a snow scene from a calendar or magazine to show to the children.

What did you think when you looked outside and saw the snow this morning? Do the places where you play look different today? I think the bushes look like giant popcorn balls.

Do you like to play in the snow? What do you like to do in snow? *(Make snow angels, snowballs, snowmen; sled; ski; shovel it.)*

Can you think of anything else in nature that is as white as snow? *(An Easter lily, a cloud, cotton, wool, ice.)* I can't think of anything that looks as pure white as freshly fallen snow.

When we first see the snow, it looks like frosting or icing on the houses, streets, trees, and cars. It looks clean and white. Maybe you know a fairy tale about a girl named Snow White. When we start to play or walk or drive cars in the snow, what happens to its whiteness? The snow, especially on the roads, doesn't stay clean, white, and beautiful. It becomes dirty and messy.

Do you think we can find anything in the Bible about clean and dirty snow? I found in the book of Samuel, a story about King David. David loved God, but sometimes David did wrong things. He took another man's wife and murdered her husband. David knew God's laws. He knew that he had broken the Ten Commandments.

Do you always know what is right and what is wrong? Sometimes it's hard to know. But, when we do something that is against the way God says we should live, we know that is wrong. We call those wrong, evil things "sin."

Sometimes we know what we have done is wrong, but we don't want to say so. Have you ever borrowed or played with a toy that belonged to your sister or brother without first asking if you may? How would you feel if you broke it? Would you want to tell anyone what happened?

David thought he could keep his terrible sin a secret, but God knew. God was not pleased with what David had done. God sent Nathan to tell King David that he had done evil; he had not obeyed God's laws.

Listen to what David told Nathan. *(Read aloud 2 Samuel 12:13a.)* David admitted his sin. He was unhappy that he had brought sadness to God. This is what David wrote about that time. *(Read aloud Psalm 51:2 and 7b.)* Did you hear the word "snow"? *(Read again.)* David asked God to take away his sin. He asked God to wash him, to make him clean and whiter than snow. David asked God to do something else. Listen. *(Read Psalm 51:10.)* David asked God to give him a clean heart and a right spirit so that he would no longer want to do things against God's way.

It was wrong for David to take another man's wife and to have her husband killed. Even so, God forgave David because David was truly sorry for what he had done. God didn't like what David had done, but God loved David.

Is there anyone here today who has never done anything wrong? We are not perfect people. We can't please God by ourselves. We need God's help. Sometimes God uses a minister, a parent, or a teacher to help us to understand, to show or tell us that we have sinned, just as Nathan told David.

When you have done something wrong, something that you know makes God unhappy, what should you do? If you have hurt or been unkind to someone, you need to tell that person you are sorry. Is there anyone else you should tell? You should tell God that you are sorry, too, and ask God to forgive you. God loves you. God forgives, and God washes you whiter than fresh, clean snow. Think about a time when you were hot, dirty, or sticky. Then you had a bath or a shower. Wasn't it a good feeling all over to be clean again? With your clean heart and the help of your parents, your teachers, and the Word of God, you can grow and learn to do things God's way.

Who expects to play in the snow today? I hope the snow will make you think about how much God loves you. God loves you enough to make you whiter than freshly fallen snow.

OPTIONAL: STRETCHING FURTHER
Read aloud Mark 4:26–29. Compare the continual, gradual growing of the seed and the plant to the way we grow in our understanding of God and the way God wants us to live, loving one another.

Let's pray. (*Ask children to bow their heads and repeat after you.*)

Dear God, thank you for the beautiful snow. Thank you for loving us. Help us to grow and learn to do things your way. We pray in Jesus' name. Amen.

24
No Expiration Date

THEME: God's offer of salvation has no expiration date.

SCRIPTURE: For God so loved the world that he gave his only Son, so that everyone who believes in him may not perish but may have eternal life.—John 3:16

PREPARATION: 1. Gather manufacturer's coupons for items of food. One coupon should say "no expiration date." The other coupons should have expired before today. Be sure to have one coupon per child. 2. Gather various ads showing different offers of rebates, cash back, and so on.

Thanksgiving Day will soon be here. Are you going to spend at least part of the day with relatives that you don't see very often? I'm looking forward to my family being together.

*I've been planning what we shall eat on Thanksgiving Day. Do you have favorite foods you like to eat on Thanksgiving Day? I looked at the grocery store ads to get some ideas. I'm a bargain hunter, so if something I want to serve for dinner is cheaper at one store than at another, I will probably buy our food at the place with the best price. I found some coupons that say I can save forty cents, or fifty-five cents, or one dollar on different foods that I might want to buy. (*Give a coupon to each child.*) Maybe you can help me to decide which coupons I should use. (*Ask each child to look at the picture on the coupon and name the item of food.*) Would you like it as part of your Thanksgiving dinner? How much money can I save if I use the coupon? (*Assist children as necessary.*)

(*After foods have been named, ask children to return the coupons to you.*) Thank you for helping me to plan my special dinner. (*Look *closely at returned coupons.)* Oh, no! This coupon expired in August! That means it's too late. I can't use it. I hope it's the only one that's expired. Oh, dear! This one expired in September. *(Look through all the coupons, finding that all but one have expired.)* Oh, this one says "no expiration date." That means I can use it any time. I'm glad. I'll save a little bit of money.

Have you seen or heard other kinds of offers that people make to get you to buy what they're selling? Sometimes a sign says "Buy one; get one free." *(If available, show additional ads with words such as, "Cash Back," "Instant Rebates," "Big Toy Blowout," or "Clearance.")*

There are many ways that we can save money and use it wisely. But we need to be careful. If a new bicycle has a tag on it with a very low price, it isn't a bargain for you if you don't need a new bike.

Would you believe that I found in the Bible the greatest offer I will ever find? It's an offer from God. Listen to what Jesus said about it. *(Read aloud John 3:16.)* Who is God's only son? This offer from God is for everyone who believes in Jesus. God offers us eternal life—living forever in Heaven with Jesus after our bodies die.

Did you hear an expiration date in God's offer? Listen again. *(Reread John 3:16.)* Is God's offer good only for a certain amount of time? No! It's never too late to accept Jesus and be given life that lasts forever. Did you hear how much you have to pay? God's offer is free! We don't have to buy it. What a bargain! But it isn't cheap. Jesus paid for it. He bought it for us when he died on the cross for us.

God's offer of eternal life saves us from having to pay for what we have done wrong. The word "Savior" comes from the word "save." God knew that we needed a Savior, so God sent Jesus to save us. God didn't send Jesus to judge or punish us. God's son came to earth so that people could believe in him, trust him, and have eternal life.

I found God's offer to save us in the third chapter of the Gospel of John. A shorter way to say that is John 3:16. Say it with me: "John 3:16." This verse tells the greatest message there is—love. It is from the greatest power there is—God. It tells about the greatest sacrifice ever made—Jesus, God's son. God's offer is for everyone, and everyone needs it. It's important that we know this message. Please repeat after me. *(Say the scripture in four or five phrases, pausing for the children to repeat.)*

I'm going to give back to each of you an expired, outdated coupon. Why do you think I'm doing that? You can't "spend" the coupons. I want you to put the coupon in your pocket to remind you of John 3:16. How about asking your parents to help you practice saying this verse? The next time we meet, we'll try saying it together. Remember that God loves everyone so much that he gave Jesus to save us. God loves you with the greatest love there is. God's love never runs out; it's good all the time and forever. I hope the coupon will remind you.

OPTIONAL: STRETCHING FURTHER

Ask children what things they want to say thank you to God for. If necessary, remind them that we should thank God for all that we have, including God's love, Jesus, families, friends, teachers, food, a place to live, clothing, rain, sunshine, and so on.

Let's pray. (*Ask children to bow their heads and repeat after you. Say short, meaningful phrases.*)

Dear God, thank you for this wonderful day. Thank you for loving everyone. Most of all, thank you for sending your son Jesus to save us and let us live forever with him. We pray in Jesus' name. Amen.

25
King of Kings

THEME: Jesus Christ is the Ruler whom God promised to send from David's family.

SCRIPTURE: But you, O Bethlehem of Ephrathah, who are one of the little clans of Judah, from you shall come forth for me one who is to rule in Israel, whose origin is from old, from ancient days.—Micah 5:2

PREPARATION: Notice any banners, signs, cloths, and windows showing symbols, such as a crown, depicting Christ as Ruler. Bookmark passages of scripture to be read aloud: 1 Samuel 8:5; 2 Samuel 7:16; Micah 5:2. You may also want to mark the first pages of Judges and 1 Samuel to show to the children.

Today we are going to talk about kings. Have you ever heard or read a story about a king? I remember a story about a king named Midas. I remember King Midas because everything he touched turned to gold.

What things do you think of when you think of a king? What does a king wear? (*A crown, a robe.*) Where does a king live? (*In a palace.*) What kind of chair does a king sit on? (*A throne.*) What might a king hold in his hand? (*A scepter or a spear.*) In Bible times, how did a king travel from his palace to another place? (*In a royal chariot.*)

Are there kings today? Do we have a king in this country? What do you think is the job of a king? A king rules over his people.

Are there any kings we can read about in the Bible? (*Children may have heard of King David, Saul, Solomon, or Herod.*) The people of Israel had kings ruling over them a long time ago, but they didn't always have kings. Before kings, God chose leaders for them called judges. A judge led the army in fighting enemies, and he was a hero to the people. A judge was like a governor, too, in charge of the government.

We can read about the judges over Israel in the book of the Bible called "Judges." (*Show Bible opened to the first chapter of Judges.*) One of the judges was Samuel, who was also a prophet. Do you know what a prophet is? A prophet is someone whom God uses to tell God's messages to the people. A prophet speaks for God.

When Samuel became old, he made his sons judges, too, but Samuel's sons were not good judges like their father. Listen to what the people said to Samuel. (*Read aloud 1 Samuel 8:5.*) What did the people want instead of judges? They wanted a king, such as other nations had.

We learn in the book of 1 Samuel (*Show Bible opened to the first chapter of 1 Samuel.*) that God chose a tall, handsome, young man named Saul to be Israel's first king. After Saul, God chose David to be king. We call King David the greatest king of Israel. Listen to what God's prophet Nathan told King David. (*Read aloud 2 Samuel 7:16.*) God promised that David's house—his family—would rule forever.

Many years later, God spoke to the prophet Micah. God told Micah where to look for this king who will "be great to the ends of the earth" (*read aloud Micah 5:2*). Jerusalem is the capital city of Israel, like Washington, D.C., is the capital city of the United States. The president lives in our capital city, but Jerusalem is not where the people of Israel were to find their ruler. The promised ruler was to come as a baby in a tiny town called Bethlehem.

God also told the prophet Isaiah that the ruler would come from the family of David, as God had promised hundreds of years ago. This promised ruler was to rule forever and bring peace to the people of God.

Many years had passed again, but the ruler had not come. Again, God spoke to a prophet—Jeremiah. God told Jeremiah, too, that a ruler would come from the family of David. This ruler would do what is fair and right.

Do you know that this ruler has come? Do you know who this ruler is? Jesus is the ruler God promised. Jesus Christ is the branch from David's family tree. More than five hundred years had passed since a ruler from David's family had ruled in Jerusalem, until Jesus came to live among people on earth. He came, according to God's plan, to show how much God loved all of them. Jesus Christ is the Ruler who leads those who believe in him.

Today we look ahead to what will happen. We will celebrate Jesus' birthday. He was not born in a palace with a throne and a crown. He didn't wear expensive clothes or ride in a royal chariot. But when the wise men were looking for him, they asked, "Where is the child who has been born King of the Jews?"

We know that Jesus rules now in heaven. We look forward to the time when Jesus will come again to be our King of kings, to rule forever in a realm of peace.

As we prepare to celebrate Jesus' birthday at Christmastime, we will sing songs that Christians have been singing for hundreds of years. Can you think of any songs that tell about Jesus Christ the King? (*In "Silent Night, Holy Night," we sing "Alleluia to our king." In "Hark! The Herald Angels Sing!" we sing, "Glory to the newborn king." In "What Child Is This?" we sing, "This, this is Christ the king." In "Joy to the World!" we sing "Let earth receive her king." In "Who Is He in Yonder Stall?" we sing "'Tis the Lord! The King of glory! At his feet we humbly fall, Crown him! Crown him, Lord of all!"*) I hope that you will listen for words about Jesus Christ the King in songs and Bible stories about Jesus.

OPTIONAL: STRETCHING FURTHER
(*Read aloud 2 Kings 11:21.*) Do we have any seven-year-olds here today? Can you imagine being a king when you are only seven years old? That's what happened to Jehoash. How do you think he knew what to do? (*A priest instructed him. God guided Jehoash in leading the country.*)

Let's pray. (*Remind children to bow their heads and repeat after you. Say short, meaningful phrases.*)

Dear God, we are glad that you keep your promises. Thank you for sending Jesus to us. Help us to obey you and do what is right, as we wait for Jesus to come again. We pray in the name of Jesus Christ, our Ruler and King. Amen.

26
What Makes Christmas Special?

THEME: God became like us so we could see how to be like God.

SCRIPTURE: "Do not be afraid, Mary, for you have found favor with God. And now, you will conceive in your womb and bear a son, and you will name him Jesus."—Luke 1:30b-31
"The child to be born will be holy; he will be called the Son of God."—Luke 1:35b

PREPARATION: Clip colorful ads for Christmas gifts or decorations. Obtain small, individual birthday cake candles to give one to each child.

A special, wonderful time of year will soon be here. What is that special time? Yes, Christmas is coming. What makes Christmas special? (*Expect children to mention presents, Santa Claus, decorations, a tree, cookies, and cards.*)

Do you like having vacation from school? How about traveling to visit friends and family who live far away? Are there special foods that your family enjoys? What about music? What do we sing about at Christmastime?

At this time of year, the stores are very busy with people buying presents for one another. The stores advertise what they have for sale so that shoppers will buy from them. (*Show clipped ad or circular.*) *This ad was delivered to my house along with the Sunday newspaper. What do you see on this ad? (*Bright colors, especially green and red;*

gift wrap; tape; plastic cups, plates and utensils; Christmas cards; candy canes; lights; batteries; candles.) I see some words in big letters near the top of the ad. Can you read them? The words say, "WE MAKE CHRISTMAS SPECIAL!"

We have talked about many things that are fun at Christmastime. Whose birthday will we celebrate on Christmas Day? Christmas is like a birthday party for Jesus. Why do we make it such a big celebration that we spend weeks in getting ready for it? *(There is nothing else in history, since time began, that can compare with God's son being born on earth.)*

Have you ever been in a play or a program where you memorized what you were supposed to say? Maybe you will do that for a program here at church or at school. Usually, a few people are onstage or up front, acting out and telling a story. The director has them practice again and again until they know what to do and what to say. Then, when the actors put on the play for friends and family and the rest of the congregation, the director usually stays behind a curtain or somewhere the audience can't see her or him. The director is invisible to the audience, but the actors know that the director is there to help them if they forget their parts.

I think of God as being the director of the universe. God is the One in charge of everything and everybody in it. God has the "playbook," *(lift the Bible.)* the program that tells us what to say and do. God is invisible to us, but God sees that we don't always follow the book. We don't act the way God wants us to act.

Because God loves us so much, God showed us how to live. God, in person, stepped onto the stage. Do you know what God did? Listen to the gospel according to Luke. The angel Gabriel speaks to Mary. *(Read aloud Luke 1:30b–31, and 35b.)* God stepped onstage when Jesus arrived on earth as a baby boy, God's child, born to Mary.

The baby Jesus, the Messiah, grew up to be a man who showed us how to live. This is what he said. *(Read aloud Matthew 22:37–39.)* What does God want us to do? Jesus said that you should love God with all your *(pause for children to speak with you)* "heart," and with all your *(pause)* "soul," and with all your *(pause)* "mind." *(Repeat if you wish.)* The second part of what Jesus said tells us to love your *(pause)* "neighbor" as yourself.

If we should forget and we don't know what to do, we can go to the "playbook." *(Lift the Bible.)*

There is something else we can do when we don't know what to do. When we need help, we can talk with the director. How can we talk to One who is invisible? (*We can pray.*)

It isn't toys, food, shopping, and vacation from school that make Christmas special. What makes Christmas special is that God became like us so we could see how to be like God. It is the gift of Jesus Christ to us that we celebrate. No matter who we are or what we have done, God's love is for us if we open our hearts to receive the gift.

Here is something to remind you that Christmas is special because it's Jesus' birthday. (*Hand out candles.*) We will celebrate God's coming to Earth as a baby.

You might want to put this candle on a cake or a cupcake at home, in honor of Jesus' birthday, but please don't try to light this candle. It's dangerous for you to do that by yourself. You could get hurt. Please talk to your parents if you think you want to see the candle lit.

OPTIONAL: STRETCHING FURTHER

Another name we sometimes call Jesus is Emmanuel, which means "God is with us." Emmanuel is a name we sing in some Christmas songs. (*Refer to "O Come, O Come, Emmanuel" and the last verse of "O Little Town of Bethlehem." A song that children and congregation could sing together is "Emmanuel, Emmanuel," by Bob McGee.*)

Let's pray. (*Ask children to bow their heads and repeat after you. Say short, meaningful phrases.*)

Dear God, thank you for sending the baby Jesus to us. Help us to remember that the gift of your child is what makes Christmas special. We want to live the way he showed us. In his name. Amen.

Bibliography

ABCs of the Bible: Intriguing Questions and Answers about the Greatest Book Ever Written. Pleasantville, N.Y.: Reader's Digest Association, 1991.

Asimov, Isaac. *Isaac Asimov's Book of Facts.* New York: Random House, 1997.

Brown, Margaret Wise. *The Runaway Bunny.* Illus. Clement Hurd. New York: Harper, 1942.

Brown, Robert K., and Mark R. Norton, eds. *The One Year Book of Hymns.* Wheaton, Ill.: Tyndale House, 1995.

Burnette, Melanie M. *365 Bible Prayers for Children.* New York: Testament Books, 2000.

Dallas Seminary Faculty. *The Bible Knowledge Commentary: An Exposition of the Scriptures.* Ed. John F. Walvoord and Roy B. Zuck. Wheaton, Ill.: Victor Books, 1985.

Egermeier, Elsie E. *Bible Story Book: A Complete Narration from Genesis to Revelation for Young and Old.* Anderson, Ind.: Warner Press, 1939.

Fellowship Songs. Dayton, Ohio: Board of Christian Education of Evangelical United Brethren Church, nd.

Galli, Mark, and James S. Bell Jr. *The Complete Idiot's Guide to Prayer.* Indianapolis, Ind.: Alpha Books, 1999.

Holy Bible: International Children's Bible, New Century Version. Dallas, Texas: Word Publishing, 1988.

Holy Bible: New Revised Standard Version Bible. National Council of the Churches of Christ in the United States of America. Grand Rapids, Mich.: Zondervan, 1989.

Life Application Bible: New International Version. Wheaton, Ill.: Tyndale House; Grand Rapids, Mich.: Zondervan, 1991.

Miller, Madeleine S., and J. Lane Miller. *The New Harper's Bible Dictionary.* New York: Harper & Row, 1973.

Praises for Children. Dallas, Texas: Stamps-Baxter Music of Zondervan, nd.

Touching the Father's Heart: Before You Now Songbook. Anaheim, Calif.: Mercy/Vineyard, 1994.

United Methodist Hymnal. Nashville, Tenn.: United Methodist Publishing House, 1989.

The World Book Encyclopedia. Chicago: World Book Inc., 2000.

Index

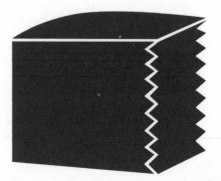